A Grand Metamorphosis

Sunday afternoon :

Education and instruction out of insight into the necessary new form of life : a new art of education is necessary.

The state, when it determines the goals of education, cannot help but influence its citizens at the same time.

The human being must fit into a new life. One must teach out of knowledge of the human being, love of the human being, and out of an art of education for the human being.

The human evolutionary epochs.

Rudolf Steiner's notebook entry (archive no. 57) for the lecture of August 31, 1919 (afternoon)

A Grand Metamorphosis

Contributions to the Spiritual-Scientific
Anthropology and Education of Adolescents

Peter Selg

2008
SteinerBooks

SteinerBooks
834 Main Street, PO Box 358, Spencertown, NY 12165
www.steinerbooks.org

Copyright 2008 by Peter Selg. All rights reserved. No part of this publication may be reproduced, stored in a retrieval system, or transmitted, in any form or by any means, electronic, mechanical, photocopying, recording, or otherwise, without the prior written permission of the publisher.

Translated by Margot M. Saar.
Notes translated by Anna R. Meuss.

Original published in German by Verlag am Goetheanum as *Eine grandiose Metamorphose. Zur geisteswissenschaftlichen Anthropologie und Pädogogik des Jugendalters.*

Library of Congress Cataloging-in-Publication Data

Selg, Peter, 1963-
 [Grandiose Metamorphose. English]
 A grand metamorphosis : contributions to the spiritual-scientific anthropology and education of adolescents / Peter Selg.
   p. cm.
 ISBN 978-0-88010-598-9
 1. Adolescent psychology. 2. Waldorf method of education. 3. Education—Philosophy. 4. Steiner, Rudolf, 1861-1925. I. Title.
 BF724.S398713 2008
 155.5—dc22
                                              2008038009

Printed in the United States of America
by Integrated Books International

dedicated to

The Independent Waldorf Schools
in memory of Rudolf Steiner

Contents

INTRODUCTION   9

1. *"A grand metamorphosis"*
   On the Constellation of Forces in Adolescence   15

2. *"We must make the cause true from the inside."*
   Qualities of an Education for Adolescents   35

3. *"The teachers completely lost touch with the high school students."*
   Rudolf Steiner's Criticism of the Teachers at the First Waldorf School in Stuttgart   49

ADDENDA

RUDOLF GROSSE: *"Your teachers think day and night about what your future will be like."*
Rudolf Steiner and the First Graduates of the Stuttgart Waldorf School, 1924   63

EUGEN KOLISKO: *"The present world situation"*
Speech Given at a Reunion of Former Waldorf Students, October 13, 1930   69

ITA WEGMAN: *"We fight for each soul."*
Letter to Ernst Lehrs Concerning the Education of Adolescents, January 20, 1931   83

NOTES   87
LITERATURE CITED   121
ABOUT THE ITA WEGMAN INSTITUTE   127

It is a matter of summarizing all education and teaching [for adolescents] in a basic feeling so that you can, in a way, sense in your soul the powerful impact of this task: we have to place the young people right into the world. Without that, our [Waldorf] school will be an empty phrase. We might say all sorts of beautiful things about our school, but we will walk on a ground that is full of holes, and eventually, the holes will become so big that there is no ground left to walk on.

We have to make the cause true from the inside.

RUDOLF STEINER, JUNE 17, 1921 (302, 94 F.)[1]

When we speak about Dr. Steiner's relationship to the Waldorf School we have to include many personal and intimate things from the Waldorf School. After all, people have a right to hear about these things.

CAROLINE VON HEYDEBRAND, 1927[2]

Introduction

Much is said here about the principles of the Waldorf School, about a new education. What is most important is that we keep developing it. Every day there is a danger that things turn sour. —That is the important thing: that people do not fall asleep because they are stuck in their habits when they have to do or work on something. (217a, 184 f.)

THE FOLLOWING ESSAY is the revision of a lecture about spiritual-scientific aspects of an anthropology and education for adolescents that I was invited to give on November 13, 2004, in the Steiner School in Freiburg-Wiehre, Germany.

The purpose of my lecture was not so much to speak as a physician specializing in child and youth psychiatry about the particular situation in which young people find themselves at the beginning of the twenty-first century, or about the special characteristics of this generation and dangers to which they are exposed. I wanted rather to use Rudolf Steiner's work to highlight the fundamental structure of the crisis[3] of adolescence and the pedagogical challenges that emerge as a result. My intention was to look at and draw attention to the particular intensity and clarity of Steiner's statements and views on this topic. They have clearly hardly lost any of their relevance today, as many issues related to the foundation of the Stuttgart Waldorf School remain open or unaddressed. The minutes taken at the faculty meetings show that Steiner's last meeting with the faculty in

August 1924, as well as many meetings in the years before that, were determined by, at times, severe difficulties that prevented the implementation of the education for puberty and adolescence which he had envisaged. The difficulties were not about the differentiated or age-specific teaching contents developed by Steiner, nor were they entirely about the intended work and further development projects that failed, partly due to a lack of funding. More often than not, the difficulties were due to the behavior of individual teachers and their attitude toward the young people: they were about the lack of an understanding of adolescence—the lack of an anthroposophical-anthropological insight necessary for an adequate (i.e., self-questioning and continuously developing) attitude or personality on the part of the teacher. In this situation, Rudolf Steiner planned to give further developmental courses for the faculty of teachers in Stuttgart. He became ill, however, and died at the end of March 1925, and the courses never took place. The faculty meetings of the Stuttgart Waldorf School end with this circumstance, which can be seen as disillusioning but also as an urgent legacy.

The questions and tasks that Rudolf Steiner raised in those faculty meetings clearly still exist today, albeit in a modified, even aggravated way, and they are waiting to be addressed. It is evident that working with children in the phase of adolescence makes special demands on teachers. These demands cannot be met by appealing to anthroposophy or to any other theories. They question the teachers—their genuine knowledge of the world, their maturity and authenticity; but also their pedagogical willingness to engage in a meeting that is based on real interest, and that will ultimately lead them to acknowledge and bear the inner abyss which separates them, with their life experience, from the situation of the adolescents that they see in front of them. In the autumn of 1924, Rudolf Steiner wanted to speak about the ethics of a future education for adolescents and to give new impulses to this end. One can assume that he would have spoken about what is necessary for an education that does not only try to place young people into the present world and civilization, but that anticipates and encourages the powers of the future that are definitely present in them.

The following presentation, which follows Rudolf Steiner's words closely and contains many actual quotations, presupposes that Steiner's existing comments on education and physiological development supply aspects that are essential for establishing a necessary pedagogical ethics for adolescence—as long as they are not merely expected to be "known" in anthroposophical circles, but have actually been fundamentally understood and internalized. If we concentrate on Steiner's individual and consistently accurate comments, and refer them to the experiences to which we have access, individually decisive changes can unfold, in knowledge as well as in practice.

At the same time, I am aware that this short book and the lecture it is based on are, by necessity, aphoristic in character; much has been abbreviated and intentionally condensed. It is meant as a specific inspiration and must be seen in context with Rudolf Steiner's pedagogical and anthropological work, and also with the rich and substantial literature on the youth question that exists inside and outside of Waldorf education. This literature is worth studying, even if it can occasionally lead away from the existential-essential and innovative-impulsive reality of Steiner's presence in the Stuttgart Waldorf School[4] that constitutes the content of the following pages. I would like to mention Erhard Fucke's exemplary work on Rudolf Steiner's conception of a curriculum for puberty and adolescence,[5] as well as Karl-Martin Dietz's various fundamental studies, including his work on Rudolf Steiner's ideas concerning self-reliance in adolescence.[6]

My contribution begins with a contemplation of the physiological developmental shift that marks the onset of adolescence, the foundation for which has to be laid during the first two seven-year periods. When contemplating the much-discussed phenomena of puberty and adolescence we must not forget that any evident youth crisis has to be seen and understood in connection with the development and the omissions that led up to it. Adolescence leads the individual toward specific changes and challenges. Whether and how these will be mastered is not primarily determined during this actual phase, but mostly by the forces and conditions that were established during the first two seven-year periods (*"We will carry these in us later on. We always carry everything in us."* 218, 325). This manuscript concludes with three contributions that all touch on the theme of anticipating the future in the present. The first is an invaluable recollection of Rudolf Steiner's last two meetings with the first graduates of the Free Waldorf School, in which the young people spoke about their future plans and their concerns. The later testimonials by Ita Wegman and Eugen Kolisko, both physicians and school doctors who had worked closely with Rudolf Steiner on educational questions and who continued to work in this spirit, are imbued with a forward-looking and, I think, still-exemplary endeavor to prepare young people for their destinies and to place them firmly *"into the world,"* which must not be misunderstood as meaning that they should be encouraged to adapt to the world as they find it. Not only the Free Waldorf Schools and the young people themselves, but human civilization as a whole, depend on the achievement of this educational aim for their future.

*

I would like to thank Peter Mathiessen, the inspiring and instructive founder and leader of the youth psychiatry department of the Herdecke Hospital in Germany, with whom I had the privilege of working from 1993 to 2000; also my fellow physicians Peter Sailer, Ilka Deppe, and Peter Milek, and the entire staff of ward "Station 4 Ost." Together we worked through many severe crisis situations with the young people entrusted to us. Neither these experiences nor the secondary literature listed in the bibliography are the explicit subject of this work, but they played a part in directing my attention toward the forces of adolescence and their constellation in health, illness, and healing, as well as toward Rudolf Steiner's conceptual explication of this in his work on developmental physiology, and also the different kinds of omissions and individual failures that occurred in the work with young people—also in the practice of Waldorf education. We can appreciate the often excellent work that has been and is being done in Waldorf schools without denying the problems of adolescence—or with the being of an individual adolescent (Dietz),[6a]—that emerged in Rudolf Steiner's time and that still emerge today. It is essential that these problems and the challenges they pose are penetrated even more deeply, taken on wholeheartedly, and approached with the future in mind. Endeavors in this direction are being made, in line with what Fucke[7] describes as the "continuous intentions of Waldorf education," with positive results.[8]

PETER SELG

Director of the Ita Wegman Institute
for Basic Research into Anthroposophy

1.

"A grand metamorphosis"

On the Constellation of Forces in Adolescence

> With sexual maturity something entirely new sets in. Afterward, the adolescent is a completely different being. (303, 236)

IN THE COURSE OF HUMAN DEVELOPMENT, adolescence stands out as a time of crises and transitions. The risks, and the new dimensions of freedom introduced thereby, form a unique part of the individual biography and bring about—even equate to—the true beginning of responsible earthly existence. According to Rudolf Steiner, the spirit-soul descends from cosmic heights and outer spheres and reincarnates into the bodily organization beginning with the maturation of the senses,[9] which follows the embryonic and fetal stages inside the womb and stretches over the first seven years of earthly life. During this time the soul, even the entire organization of the child, is fully exposed to, and takes in, all the processes that occur in the surrounding world. What we see here is a continuation of the spiritual imitation and replication processes of pre-earthly, cosmic existence.[10] Physiologically, the nerve-sense system,[11] (i.e., the upper pole of the human organism) ripens during this time; the individuality takes hold of it gradually, in strict progress from the top downward. During the first seven years of life the child is all sense organ, as Rudolf Steiner described with recurring emphasis and in ever more detail.[12] The child feels an unlimited and genuine trust in the surrounding world, and in the people who are directly related, experiencing the world as personified in these people, and living in *their* world—gradually becoming part of it, in a physical as well as a moral sense.

With the change of teeth, children come to a definite transformation as physiological incarnation and soul development now start favoring the rhythmical system,[13] which represents the middle of the human organization.[14] Although they are still essentially carried by their surroundings, they now increasingly experience their inner soul-space and develop a feeling of self-awareness. Living entirely out of the forces of the developing heart-breathing-system or *breathing maturity* and permeated by etheric health forces, they tentatively begin to experience themselves, internalizing their experience of the world, which previously was entirely outwardly directed, and find themselves in the realm of feeling—whether outer conditions are favorable, or also in spite of deeply irritating or traumatic circumstances. Having arrived in the "middle of childhood" as well as in the middle of their own organism,[15] they are now preparing the way into adolescence, the next step into earthly life, that leads from the beauty and harmony[16] of the second seven-year-period—previously inwardly and outwardly experienced—to individual morality, which begins to shape and prove itself through their struggles and conflicts with the surrounding world. While their muscles were still intimately connected with the rhythmic processes of respiration and blood circulation during the middle of childhood, which resulted in a completely harmonious movement gesture, they orientate themselves now, with beginning earthly maturity, toward the skeleton (*"Now the muscles turn away from their intimate closeness to breathing and circulation and toward the bone system, the skeleton. From now on they adapt to the skeleton."* 303, 204)—a physiological process which signifies that the individuality is breaking through into a sphere governed by earthly laws:

> ... The human being works through the breathing and circulation system down to where the muscles are connected to the bones, working toward the outer periphery and breaking through into the outer world when sexual maturity is reached. Only now does the human being fully stand in the outer world. (303, 238)

Only when this stage in the incarnating process has been reached can the human spirit-soul truly relate to earthly conditions and actually integrate what is of the earth into its organization. In doing this, it also experiences what is inorganic and causal: compulsion and death. On January 19, 1922, Rudolf Steiner said in a lecture, after having given an overview of the first two seven-year-periods:

> What is most active in the child? It is the brain! From the brain the plastic formation of the whole body radiates outwards. It is most active up to the change of teeth. When the teeth change, this formative power is passed on to the respiration-heat-system, and until puberty this system takes over.... Between the seventh and fourteenth years, the muscles develop in accordance with the rhythmic system. Only when the child approaches the fourteenth year does the spirit-soul take hold of the whole human being. It is interesting to observe how the muscles were previously oriented toward heartbeat, pulse and breathing. Now they begin to befriend the bones, the skeleton, through the tendons adapting to the outer movement.... Starting from the head, the soul grows more and more toward the periphery, using up the human being, getting closer and closer to the death forces until they take over in the moment of death. (210, 233 ff.)

What Steiner describes as a *"growing into the earth forces"* (348, 55), or *befriending the earth and death forces,* young people are compelled to do physiologically right down into their physical body. This *"grand metamorphosis"* of their existence (303, 242) presents, despite the fact that it has been prepared in their physiological development, a radical loss of the spirit-soul world that has carried them up until now:

> It is no exaggeration, but the actual truth to say that with sexual maturity human beings are cast out of the spiritual world and into the external world.... Young people might not have a conscious awareness of this, but in the subconscious it plays an even bigger, more intense part. In the subconscious, human beings compare the world that they are entering now—subconsciously or half-consciously—with the world that they formerly had within them. Previously, they were not consciously aware that they had it within themselves, but they had an inner way of working with it. In their inner life, human beings are able to work freely with the higher world, with the soul-spiritual world. The external world offers no such provision. Here we are confronted with all kinds of hindrances, and, at the same time, with the wish to overcome these hindrances. A tumultuous situation arises in the relationship between the adolescent of fourteen or fifteen to twenty-one years and the world. This tumultuous situation is necessary, and as teachers we need to have it in mind already during the years leading up to it. Overly sensitive teachers might get the idea that it would be better to spare young people this inner upheaval. But in doing so they would make themselves into the worst enemy of youth. (303, 238 ff.)

In just the same way as the maturing nerve-sense and rhythmical systems dominated the development of the first two seven-year periods, the metabolic-limb system now unfolds, as earthly organization and will-carrier, to its full potential. The metabolic-limb system,[17] as will-organization (Steiner), breaks through physiologically: young people leave the protection of a predominantly harmonious inner space and arrive at the point where they have to meet and come to terms with outer forces. This time cannot be postponed; any retardation or distortion would be pathological. Their will potential is no longer tied to and absorbed by the physical organization, but is partly set free. This is necessary for them in order to find a new will-based relationship with the world, and to be able to form ideals that can inspire them to become active. Physiologically, a definite restructuring of inner forces occurs: according to Steiner, the metabolic-limb system's increased desire and will-forces are integrating into the organism, virtually radiating through it from below upward, rising up to permeate the body. In an emerging balance of systems, forces, and processes, they constitute the physiological situation of health and illness for the time of *earthly maturity*.[18] At the same time, the rising forces and processes cause a necessary "congestion"; through this, the rhythmic organization and the larynx-speech area[19] can become ensouled, and can bring about a change of the entire instrument and potential of speech.

> One learns to recognize how the soul-spirit manifests in the outer physical body, and one learns to recognize how the will-nature finds its place in the nature of the larynx; one learns to observe how the will shoots into speech. (301, 23)

> The change of voice is something that is forced onto the human being from the outside; it places the human being's innermost being into the outer world. It is not just that the soft parts of the larynx develop a tendency toward the bones: in actual fact, a slight ossification of the larynx itself takes place, which means that the larynx moves from

being part of the inner human being to being part of the physical world. (303, 242 ff.)

In the confrontation with the world- and earth-forces, adolescents begin to find their own speech;[20] at the same time, they are pressurized and threatened by these forces. In this way, the adolescent's speech and breathing organism, as an integral part of the rhythmic system, becomes—to a previously unknown and unexpected extent—the place of conflict between inner and outer worlds. The heart organism, which is adjacent and developmentally connected[21] to the speech organism, also undergoes a drastic change. Steiner described in detail how already during the years leading up to earthly maturity, the heart organ experiences lasting physiological transformation and restructuring processes, which ultimately, from the beginning of adolescence, enable the heart to become the organ wherein deeds and intentions are internalized. From puberty onward, deeds as well as intentions inscribe themselves, Steiner said, into the heart organism, which from this time on unfolds as the place where individual destiny can be realized.[22]

In the wider context of the human organization that works into the processes outlined above, Steiner described the *"grand metamorphosis"* that takes place during adolescence as the physiologically required, harmonious coming together of spirit-soul and the physical and etheric bodies; more concretely, as the astral body's gradual taking hold of, and consequent separating from, the organic life processes. According to Steiner, astrality begins to enter into physiological processes along the nerve fibres in the second seven-year-period. From its former function as a sheath in the outer periphery, it now contracts in a centripetal direction and finally reaches the stage of physical orientation that initiates the process of metamorphosis and liberation with the change of voice and the beginning of puberty.[23] The adolescent "lives" this complicated life process—the astral body (and the ego which is, in a way, immanent in it) senses itself in this restructuring and experiences its own struggle to connect with the physical and etheric bodies. In relation to this, Rudolf Steiner spoke of a human being bringing *"the whole subjective nature—ego and astral body—into relationship with the objective nature—ether body and physical body."* (302, 74)[24] He repeatedly pointed out that boys and girls tend to experience these processes in slightly different ways. Looking back at the differences that are already manifest during the second seven-year-period, Rudolf Steiner said, for example, on August 25, 1922, during an international pedagogical congress in Oxford:

> We already pointed out the difference between boys and girls that occurs around the tenth year. The girls grow faster, especially in height. With boys, growth is delayed until puberty when they tend to overtake the girls again.
> For someone with real insight into the human being—someone who can see the intimate interplay of spirit, soul, and body—this is very significant, because this growing, this overcoming of the earth's gravity, reveals something that is fundamental to human nature. The same is true for other events that happen at different stages of human development. Certain forces that come from the cosmos, from the outside into the human being, work between the ages of ten and fourteen more intensely on the female than on the male organism. In a sense, the female organism between ten and fourteen grows also physically into a supersensible world. You need to be aware of how extremely important this is. The female organism around the age of ten to twelve, thirteen, or fourteen grows, as an organism, into something that is spiritual. It becomes permeated by spirit at that time. This means that during this time the blood develops in a very special way in girls. During these years the blood circulation of the girl is open to the whole world. It is regulated by the universe. If one

would measure—even with physical instruments—how the ratio between pulse and breathing changes between the ages of ten and fourteen, one would obtain completely different results for boys and girls.

At thirteen or fourteen, boys begin to reveal a different being, and now they also begin to grow taller than girls. The boy makes up for what he missed earlier on, but his inner being confronts the world now in a completely different way than when he was younger. As a consequence, the boy's nervous system is now more engaged than the blood system. This means that the boy's nervous system can become more easily irritated if he is not taught in the right way. During these years the boy is deeply influenced by the language or languages he has learned. The human ideas that are held in a language or languages penetrate the boy during the time when his body is not growing so much. During this period, the world that forms his outer earthly environment begins to cause turmoil and upheaval within the boy.

One could say that something from the cosmos, from the universe, is planted into the girl at a slightly earlier age, while the earthly environment is planted into the boy through language. On the outside this manifests itself in the changing voice of the boy. The change of voice is an outer sign of the tremendous shift that takes place in the boy's whole organization. In the female organism the change of voice is only very subtle. (303, 164 ff.)

Later in the same lecture he continues:

The inner being of the boy of fourteen or fifteen years is stirred up by his outer environment: words with their meaningful content have, without his consciousness, moved into his nervous system and are stirring up his nerves. The boy does not know what to do with himself.

He has taken something in that begins to seem foreign to him, especially at this age. He is astonished about himself, but also critical and sceptical of himself. There seems to be nothing to hold on to. Someone who understands human nature knows that these strange two-legged creatures, these "anthropos" that walk on the earth, have never seemed as mysterious to any philosopher as they do now to the fifteen-year-old boy. All human soul forces are part of this mystery and the one that is furthest removed from human consciousness, the will, now virtually overruns the boy's nervous system.

It is different with girls. Especially if one strives—as one nowadays quite rightly does, because it will be necessary in the future—for emancipation of the sexes, it is important to develop an unbiased view of the differences between them. Equality can only be achieved with unbiased differentiation. And, in the same way that the boy becomes a riddle to himself, something that he marvels at, the outer world becomes a riddle for the girl. The girl has taken into herself something spiritual. The whole human being unfolds, unconsciously, inside the young girl. In the girl of fourteen or fifteen we see a young human being who marvels at the world, who finds the world mysterious, and who wants to find in the world, more than anything, the realization of inner values. During this time of life, the girl therefore often finds the outer world incomprehensible, whereas the boy finds the inner world incomprehensible. (305, 167 ff.)

A year earlier, on June 16, 1921, Rudolf Steiner had spoken to the faculty of the Stuttgart Waldorf School for the first time in detail about the processes in the human organization related to these gender-specific developmental tendencies. Making particular reference to the difference in the influence and dynamic of the ego and astral body, he said:

Now [with puberty] it is shown that the astral body is more significant in girls than in boys.[25] All through life, the astral body is more important for the female organism than for the male. The entire female organization is orientated towards the cosmos because of the astral body. Female nature reveals many secrets of the cosmos. The astral body of the woman is much more differentiated, much more finely structured than the astral body of the man, which is coarser in comparison. Between fourteen and twenty-one years the girl's ego, on the other hand, is strongly influenced by the developments that are going on in the astral body. One can observe how the girl's ego is virtually absorbed by the astral body[26] so that, when she reaches the age of twenty or twenty-one a strong countermovement takes place, a strong effort towards the ego.

This is very different in boys. The boy's astral body does not tend to absorb the ego so much. The ego remains concealed; it does not really come into force yet, and it is not influenced much by the astral body between the ages of fourteen and twenty-one. As the ego has, however, not achieved its independence yet, the boy of this age tends to become faint-hearted more easily than the girl. The girl develops a certain freedom of manners at this time and becomes more outgoing. In boys who are particularly sensitive, the special relationship between ego and astral body leads to a kind of inner withdrawal.... If a boy does not show this kind of subtle or obvious withdrawal, this can be cause for concern. (302, 74 ff.)

The processes that are working and searching for a balance within the human organization, described above, might be quite expressive in character, but they are nevertheless concealed, even from the one who is experiencing suffering and creating them. They take place under the protection of an inwardness that the person feels as shame.

This shame permeates the whole human being. The adolescents feel that they have to take something into their individual life that must not be revealed to the world. They need to conceal mysteries inside of themselves. This is the nature of shame. And it enters into the most unconscious regions of soul-spiritual life. (302, 80)

Even in adolescents who are apparently imitating what is in their surroundings and who are emphatically striving to be a part of their world, the metamorphosed sense of shame dominates the self-image to a large extent and hides the inner life, thus enabling it to continue its development behind an outer mask:

The adolescent might walk like someone else; might try to be as polite as someone else. All this is an expression of a striving to connect with the outer world, especially at this age. And it is, essentially, this sense of shame, this concealing of the inner being from the world, this withdrawal into the self, that makes the adolescent appear so different from what he or she is really like. (302, 81)

In the inner space of the soul's development, extensive changes and modifications of forces are taking place that run parallel to and are just as effective as the physiological changes. They enable the young people to change and shape their relationship to the world and to their own self. Intense processes of individuation and world discovery are happening in the thinking and willing, but also in the feeling experience of the surrounding world.

Based on the physiological and psychological development of the first two seven-year periods and their gestures of imitation and authoritative orientation (*"Nothing could be worse than to appeal too early too their judgment. [...] With the young person, learning has to come before judging. What reason *has to say to anything should only be said once all other soul forces have had their say; before that, reason should only play a mediating role. It should merely grasp what has been seen or felt and take it at face value, without any direct interference of an immature judgment."* 34, 342), the thinking capacity arises and emancipates itself during adolescence, followed by the capacity of free judgment. This intellectual maturation needs, so Steiner said, a previously consolidated *"sense of truth"* (*"There is no healthy thinking that has not been preceded by a healthy sense of truth which, in turn, is based on a natural belief in authority."* 34, 342) as well as a separation from what has been given or determined and was playfully(!) practiced during the second seven-year-period. Prerequisite for the young person's ability to think, criticize, and judge is the meeting of the astral body, which is being freed increasingly from its task of organ-formation, with the outside world from puberty onward. It is the astral body that enables the individual to turn toward and confront the world and humanity. Former beliefs and contents as such are no longer accepted due to forces of imitation or trust in authority, but they have to be explored in depth, grasped with the adolescents' own understanding, and verified in their own judgment—together with everything else that has been taken in and learned[27] up to this point.

Supporting themselves upon the incarnating gesture that has now reached the earthly structure, young people feel, according to Rudolf Steiner, as if they are *"inside what is machine-like in the bone system"* (305, 110). After having achieved earthly maturity, they demand causality and logic, and gain an intellectuality that is undeniably their own and corresponds to the biographic gesture of their earthly destiny:

> We see how the human being is by nature only able to move on to the intellectual once sexual maturity is reached—possibly even later. (81, 8 ff)

Without a doubt, much content that can only be grasped cognitively is offered to the child before adolescence, and it is quickly reproduced and seemingly "internalized"; but only now—away from a premature and often lifelong prejudice and partiality[28]—is the human being able to deal with it in an autonomous way, with a responsibility that is the basis for the capacity for freedom and, at the same time, depends on it.[29]

This potential capacity for freedom in the young person is, however, according to Rudolf Steiner, in no way the same as the ability to criticize and form judgments. It needs for its positive realization the ability to form ideals. Steiner emphasizes that the adolescent's developing astral body, which is characterized by inner upheavals, emotions, and desires, needs for its consolidation structured and authentic will-orientations of a reflective nature:

> We have to take this very seriously. Ideals, concepts that have will-character—ideals that have will-character—have to be introduced now as a firm scaffolding into the astral body. (302, 82)

Although adolescents must to a degree become distant and alienated from the soul-spiritual world that previously carried them, most of the period of adolescence is a *"tendency toward a supersensible ideal existence"* (302, 122), toward ideals and idealistic content. During and after earthly maturation, human beings acquire the ability *"to live themselves into their life dreams"* (143, 123)—a capacity that is linked to their will development and warmth organization. They gain an *"inner impulsivity"* (82, 42) and a growing, previously unknown ability to develop their own *"life's hopes and desires,"* which needs to be pedagogically fostered:

> Nothing is worse for later life than if these forces have not appeared by the age of twenty. (143, 123)

These life dreams which, *"out of themselves, give direction and aim"* (84, 262) to the young person's existence, and which can potentially transcend a dangerous self-fixation come, as Rudolf Steiner says, from the human heart; i.e., the organ of future and destiny (143, 123). They pave the way to full self-awareness, which is achieved by the age of twenty-one and ensures that the individual's life is related to a realistic yet imaginatively and creatively anticipated future. About the physiological "birth" of this kind of future imagination that develops during adolescence, Steiner said on January 4, 1922, in Dornach:

> Now, with puberty, something is enabled to unfold free soul activity; something that before was active in service of the breathing rhythm, that strove to bring rhythm into the muscular system, even into the bone system. This rhythmic force has now become free and is transformed into free receptiveness... for ideal and imaginative content. Genuine imagination is only really born out of the human being when sexual maturity is reached, when the astral body is born. This astral body is free from time and space, and able, just as in dreams, to link together past, present, and future according to inner considerations. (303, 238 ff.)

While living biographically into this ideal sphere of anticipated existence, the young person is able to develop a *"feeling for what is good"* (302, 136), which, however, also depends on the right pedagogical approach during previous developmental stages, especially in the second seven-year period. In the middle of childhood, there should arise—if fostered in the right way, physiologically orientated toward the rhythmical system—a real *sympathy* for what is moral, a tendency of the soul toward the good, which at that time still has to unfold in the personal authoritative relationship with the adult.

If we want the child before puberty to do what is good we have to "hold" the child close to ourselves. We must bring it about through our relationship with the child that the child is good. The authority of the teacher has to stand so strongly behind the child of eleven, twelve, or thirteen that the child has the feeling: if I am good now, I will please my teacher. In the same way the child will avoid doing what is wrong. The child should have the feeling that the teacher appears from nowhere in particular and is displeased. The child should sense the teacher's presence. In this way, the child should grow together with the teacher and only after reaching puberty become independent of the teacher. (302, 136)

The child of the second seven-year period can develop sympathy for what is moral and antipathy for what is evil—or, in other words, *"a moral-feeling judgment"* (218, 237)[30]—as a result of the morality that the child experiences in the life of the adult. (*"In education, morality is at first not taught, morality is lived"* 304, 177). This development is closely connected with the development of a sense of beauty. For the child in the middle of childhood, there is immanent beauty in all that is good, an aesthetic wholeness that can be marveled at and admired. The world has, for the child, an essential inner morality and beauty. For the child, this is experienced and witnessed within the adult person, who represents the world order (304a, 42). It is due to these experiences only, so Steiner said, that during adolescence a *"real inner concept of truth"* (293, 151) and an understanding for a lived morality can develop (*"Beauty has to reign during elementary school age and after; beauty as the interpreter of truth"* 217, 136).

In a number of pedagogical lectures, Rudolf Steiner emphasized that the idea of truth in the first seven years, supported by the highest cosmic trust, metamorphoses into the rhythm-related experience of beauty of the second seven years, and finally into the clear-cut, will-permeated understanding of morality and ideals of adolescence. To the teachers of the Stuttgart Waldorf School he once said:

> It is a downright sin to speak of what is true, beautiful, and good in an abstract way, without concrete indications of how they relate to the individual stages of development. (302, 137)

The existence of a thoroughly developed sense of truth or of moral-intellectual judgment in adolescence, in turn, forms the foundation for the potential—and psychologically necessary—development of a sense of duty that rises above the sphere of like and dislike, to a firm inner positivity. Rudolf Steiner explained that this sense of duty,[31] which is closely connected with morality, passes through biographically characteristic stages of metamorphosis and unfolds during adolescence out of the gratitude and love that have been internalized in the first and second seven-year periods. Now—due to the described transformation of the entire constitution of the human organization—these capacities can form the basis for the newly possible acceptance of what the individual recognizes as meaningful, necessary, and in need of realization; and these the young person is thus able to take, with love, into an active will:

> Love encompasses everything; it is the innermost incentive for action: we ought to do what we love to do. Duty should become one with love. We should love to do what we need to do. (302, 135)

> This so-called categorical imperative that stems from ancient times, from ancient-moral impulses, meets the request that humankind should more and more develop—

out of the depths of soul—the love for what is to become deed, for what is to become action. (217, 92)

A successful adolescence, in this sense, is the beginning of an ethical individualism where individuals are ensouled and motivated by the love *"that grows out of the vision of the deed that needs to be realized"* (217, 93), but where they, at the same time, become aware of the existence of true freedom in their own soul. *"We experience freedom when that which is moral is the deepest impulse of the individual human soul"* (310, 118). Only in this individual soul[32] can moral intuitions arise, after sexual maturity has been reached. Not only the future of individual processes but also, to an increasing extent, the future of social processes, depend on the existence and realization of these intuitions. *"I found myself compelled to say: the future of all human ethics will depend on the power of moral intuition becoming stronger every day. This also means that we can only get anywhere with our moral education if we increasingly strengthen the power of moral intuition within the soul; if we manage to achieve this, individuals become more and more conscious of the moral intuitions that their soul is able to bring forth.... The old intuitions were always given to whole groups of human beings. The new intuitions, which need to be developed now, have to be worked out in each individual human soul. This means that individual human beings have to be made the source of their own morality. This has to be taken out of the nothing that one finds oneself confronted with, with the help of the intuitions"* (217, 59/69). It is the task of education for adolescents—as an education in freedom and toward freedom (Dietz)—to foster the moral intentions of the young people, to help them perceive themselves *"as an awakening being"* (305, 74),[33] and to strengthen them in this way for their entire future earthly biography. *"This moment of awakening becomes the source of a power that will work throughout life"* (305, 74). This capacity for freedom in the adolescent is, as real self-experience, a deeply spiritual event, and marks the beginning of a genuine reconnection with the spiritual world. On August 29, 1922, Rudolf Steiner summed this up as follows:

> This is what all education has to aim for—to awaken these intuitions so that each human being can feel: I am not just of this earth, I am not just a product of physical heredity; I have come down to earth from the spiritual worlds, and, as the individual human being that I am, I have something to do on this earth. (305, 225)

While the powers of thinking, judging, and willing continue to unfold in the adolescent from the time of maturation, establishing an entirely new period in the individual biography, the same is true for the realization of a feeling relationship to the world. According to Rudolf Steiner the time of sexual maturation, although its soul mood is characterized by emotions and seemingly egocentric desires, reveals for the first time the adolescent's fundamental capacity for love and devotion, not just in the sense that the young person opens up to the surroundings or looks to it for guidance (as during the preceding developmental stages[34]), but in a real connection of the inner life with the inner world of another person. The unfolding of this capacity for love, Rudolf Steiner maintains, is an essential element of earthly maturity and belongs to the evolution of humankind on Earth and to its cosmic-planetary future. The connection between the sexes that begins with puberty is, in spite of all "cultural" distortions, part of and subordinate to this universal capacity for love and earthly maturity:

> With sexual maturity, young people usually develop love for everything that surrounds them. The love between man and woman is a special nuance, a particular accentuation, of universal love. Only by seeing it in this light can we rightly understand love and its task in the world. (303, 243)

During adolescence, Rudolf Steiner said, a devotional soul-force is set free and becomes active in the outer world; a power of love that before was the creative principle of the inner organization. *"What now becomes apparent on the outside is between seven and fourteen years the deepest principle of being and growth: it is, and it lives inside.... Love works inside the child and becomes outer love through sexuality."* (310, 120)[35] and thus it consists of transformed, originally natural will forces. This power of love born of puberty and adolescence often finds immediate orientation in a single other person, toward whom the entire attention (and with it all potential desire) is now directed. Rudolf Steiner, nevertheless, leaves no doubt that this youthful capacity for love stretches further and is, ultimately, not directed to one particular person, but to those human forces out of which the single person shapes an individuality. About this relationship of the growing human being to humankind as a whole, Steiner said on January 4, 1922, in connection with the first three seven-year periods:

> What is it that really happens inside human beings during sexual maturation? Up to this point one's humanity was given externally, so that one could imitate it; so that one could look up to its authority. From the outside it worked into one's being, while, conversely, one had brought everything internal from a pre-earthly existence. Humanity as a whole had worked into one's being first on the basis of imitation, then through authority. And now, as one finds one's own way to humanity, humanity does not need to work into one's being any longer in the same way as before; now a feeling for what is truly human enters one's inner being as a spiritual counterpart to the physical faculty of reproduction. Physically, one is now able to procreate. And spiritually, one becomes able to experience all of humankind within one's own self. (303, 243)

What appears in this way at the time of earthly maturity, and can continue to unfold if the right conditions prevail, is *"the feeling of social love"* (192, 193) or *"the power of love for humankind as a whole"* (296, 21), which, as such, is an essential precondition for an evolved form of human fellowship. Rudolf Steiner calls it the *"most important thing in the life of the human being."* (192, 193) However consumed the young person might be temporarily in the tumultuous upheavals of will impulses, self-doubts, and emotions—and an outside observer might well identify the young person with these—what is trying to unfold in these processes are organs of soul and spirit that are necessary for the exploration and future realization of a genuine humanity. Through entering the actual time and destiny-structure of an earthly biography,[36] adolescents acquire intuitive access to the human-moral dimension of earthly existence. They sense the momentous implications of these processes for the individual, the society, and civilization as a whole, even if they are in no way able yet to demonstrate the attitudes and actions that they experience as necessary (or that are critically demanded of them); and, in many respects, they feel themselves to be lagging behind the demands that they themselves have idealistically formulated.[37]

2.

"We have to make the cause true from the inside"
Qualities of an Education for Adolescents

> We will only be able to work in the right pedagogical way once we have acquired a certain sense of shame; once we feel ashamed when we talk about education. This might be surprising, but it is true: the way we now talk about education will be considered shameless by human beings in the future. Everybody talks about education today and about what they think is right. But education is not something that can be summarized in concepts in such a way; it cannot be grasped with theories. (217, 179 ff.)

AN EDUCATION FOR ADOLESCENTS has to do justice—in content as well as in form—to the characteristics of an extreme transition. It has to develop the "ethics" of the relation that it has established with regard to the forces and processes mentioned earlier. The *"intimacies of the art of education"* (217, 152) unfold, says Steiner, in the subtle space of an "I"-you encounter—not at all in the diffuse general human orientation, but within the margins of a situation that is characterized by a specific task, age, and relationship.

Among the many aspects that need fundamental and continuous consideration when one works pedagogically with adolescents, their radical, newly awakened capacity of critical thinking and judgment is the most noticeable (and therefore it shapes the relationship). The pedagogical challenge at this age does not, according to Rudolf Steiner, simply consist in the expectation (and, at times, relentless testing) of factual knowledge, but rather in the adolescents' search for a justification of the world and for the meaning of their own existence that comes to expression therein. Steiner repeatedly pointed out that there is a metaphysical dimension to many (posed or unposed) questions of adolescence, which includes forms of a subliminal yet existential insecurity, and possible denial of this. It is, however, not so much a matter of providing a general ontological explanation, but a concrete description of the state of the world as it is and of what it entails—not in a harmonizing, justifying way, but with regard to its inner meaning and coherence:

> [As a teacher] one has to be able to speak about the real causes of things. If young people, especially during adolescence, are led by human beings to meet a world of meaningless content, if they encounter situations in the world that make no sense and that give them the feeling: What I have experienced before I came into the world was really meaningless because it leads me into a world that is unreasonable—if they do not find adults who can, at least to a certain extent, reassure them that the world makes sense, then the inner turmoil will become too strong and the young people will lose their inner foothold, because the astral body that has become free is not of this world. Adolescents have been thrown out of the world from which they came, and are only willing to place themselves into this world if this world can justify its existence. (303, 240 ff.)

The amount of experiences that young people undergo, due to an education that bypasses them and misses its purpose, cannot be ignored. They take place subconsciously and show serious consequences: *"surging up in feelings, surging up in will impulses that become dull; living in disappointed ideals, in disappointed wishes, in a certain becoming dull toward what expresses itself in the unreasonable outer world"* (303, 241).

The apparent irrationality of the world that adolescents primarily experience requires an inner explanation that penetrates into its historical development. (*"Through the way they are taught and educated, young people have to see the outer world and its laws, its development, its causes and effects, its aims and intentions"* 302a, 76.) It therefore also requires the intellectual dissolution of existent structures and states and their reduction to their own evolutionary history, to their own structure of meaning and continuity (which is potentially accessible only retrospectively) down to the reduction of political ideologies to their philosophical and possibly biological-Darwinist theorems, which led to their development and the severe ensuing actions. There is no need for additional dogmatic bans and rigid sanctions, but again rather the need for evidence of moments and situations that preceded the existing behavior codes and that can explain them. Using the simple example of nicotine abuse among upper-school pupils of the Stuttgart Waldorf School and the strict smoking ban on school grounds that was discussed by the teachers, Rudolf Steiner pleaded for education instead of prohibition. He said during a faculty meeting:

> One explains the effect of nicotine. That is the best thing to do. [...] This example in particular shows that it is better [...] to teach the children a lesson if they get themselves into this kind of trouble. Pedagogically, you will have achieved fifteen times more this way than if you implemented a smoking ban. Implementing a smoking ban is the most convenient method. But to get the children to quit smoking out of insight, that will make a lasting difference to their lives. It is enormously important that one does not just somehow forbid and punish; that

one neither forbids nor punishes, but that one does something different. (300b, 49)

Adolescents should wake up to their own ability to form judgments and to take on responsibility out of "insight" into the circumstances that surround them. They are not meant to take on the beliefs and traditions of the teaching generation, but to learn by experience that their actions have binding consequences with which they determine the present and future shape of their social environment. Rudolf Steiner therefore called the education that is needed for adolescents an "awakening" education (304a, 178). It enables the young person to continuously wake up—a waking-up that is necessary for inner intellectual and moral independence.

*

Tuition and pedagogical guidance for adolescents should support and intellectually consolidate their spiritual grounding in the world that they have entered, and should lead to interest, insight, and potential integration. This does not mean that young people should adapt to conditions that are inhumane, morally unacceptable, or in need of change, but primarily that they become part of the anthropologic life-structures and laws, as well as the multifaceted earthly cosmos that they are incarnating into and that possesses an active spirituality to which they can gradually connect themselves. (*"[...] this experience has to lead to young people being readmitted in their twenties—equipped with everything that out of life has been impressed into them, with everything that they have impressed into life—into a world they were thrown out of during puberty. They must be re-admitted. They have to find a new connection, because without this reconnecting nothing is possible in life. This new connection they must find by themselves. If it is imposed by authority, it is of no value in later life"* 303, 241). The tuition and pedagogical guidance that are aimed at adolescents should therefore activate the forces that shape the individual's character and will and, in so doing, convey to the highly dynamic will-organization—that has been physiologically and developmentally broken up—motivation, form, and assurance to enable the young person to have an active influence and impact on the world. In his lectures on education for adolescents, Rudolf Steiner spoke repeatedly of the necessary endorsement of a real *"will culture"* (192, 93); an education of the will that would lead to initiative and genuine interest in the world; an education of the will for the future that involves activating a thinking in which the active will to achieve the capacity of free and independent judgment is of decisive importance:

> It is exactly this that, from the very beginning, has illuminated everything that lives in Waldorf education. It is not meant to be a system of principles, but a wake-up call. It should be life, not knowledge; not cleverness, but art, life-filled doing, awakening deeds. (217, 40)

It is specifically this education of the will that, together with the above-mentioned illumination of the life circumstances, enables young people to understand and commit themselves to life; no *"dropping out of time evolution"* (193, 117) but an intentional active connection to a specific present and future; an understanding that is due to experience, involvement, and openness toward the future:

> Nobody should be allowed to go through this age group without experiencing what happens in agriculture, economy, industry, and business. (192, 98)

> [...] we should awaken all that enables the human being to understand what actually has to happen in life if life is

to go on. Without that, we will always live in an environment that is unknown to us. (302, 85)

An education that enables young people to participate in many essential areas of life openly, in a cognitive-spiritual as well as volitional-active way, and to learn from life itself, does not just convey information and knowledge about numerous aspects of life and civilization (and thus free them, as Steiner says, from a *"prison without windows"*[38]) but anchors them in their own lifetime, *"the very, very closest present life"* (192, 137), which also means in their foremost sphere of incarnation and thus of their destiny, right down to its technological structures (*"The human being has to get to know the meaning of the modern technical age"*[39]). Early insights into different professional fields are therefore not just a sensible anticipation of later abilities or opportunities that help one to decide on a future professional career. They open up the *"width of the horizon for life"* (307, 244), they strengthen the social anchoring and awareness of the young people,[40] penetrating deeply into their entire organization, thus becoming their *"personal property"* (302, 86) and indispensable elements in their character and will development—but only if they can imprint an image of what is universally human into specific individuals (*"In the future, nothing should be brought to adolescents that has come from research only, that comes solely from scientific specialization, not before they have reached the age of twenty-one."* 192, 97), and if the individuals are, in themselves, as instigating and creative as they are future-orientated. A pedagogy that nurtures and gives direction to the will should support the adolescents' interest in and experience of the world, should "redeem" them from a potentially egocentric "being caught" in their own physicality and encourage them to interact creatively with the processes in their surroundings, using their moral-imaginative powers, even if this only happens in the context of an exemplary-situational activity: *"The more of the present inner life we* are able to bring to the surface, the better we support the developing human being" (55, 170).

Against the general anthropological background, this shows clearly that an education for adolescents has the task of connecting young people, on the one hand, with the (intellectually accessible) world that has become, and on the other, with a (volitionally accessible) world that is becoming, and finally, to lead them in a very deep sense into the time-relatedness of their own existence. Once they have reached puberty, adolescents meet their destiny and the chronology of their individual existence to an ever greater extent.[41] Through learning and understanding, they overtake the past, which, for its part, asserts itself more and more strongly in them. At the same time they reach out, as never before, with their will into the future, which, to start with, they help shape and gradually internalize into their own biography.

*

Ultimately, Rudolf Steiner saw the success of spiritually educating and will-activating pedagogical acts as intrinsically dependent on the individuality of the teacher *"it is of the greatest importance* who *comes to meet young people of this age as a teacher [...]"* (55, 131). The teacher's position and personality are for this age group no longer carried and supported by the forces of admiration that were active up to that time. They now have to be established on the basis of genuine knowledge and ability. (*"[...] No teacher can in truth convey any knowledge to young people, if the students have not been able to develop the feeling: My teachers know what they are talking about. It is simply irresponsible toward humankind if a teacher endeavors to work in a way that does not induce in young people the conviction: 'My teachers know what they are talking about'."* 217, 135). They have to be completely newly established and confirmed; i.e., teachers have to prove themselves in front of these very sensitive young people, not just in their ability, but in their individual integrity and credibility.[42] The teacher's position needs to carry intellectual-practical superiority, as well as differentiated insights, into the pedagogic-didactic practice. At the same time, Steiner pointed out that teachers of adolescents have to be able to establish a truly essential connection with young people and to develop a special perceptive organ for the emerging individuality of the particular person they are dealing with.[43] This means that teachers have to enter into a free encounter and relationship while their own souls are left open and continue to develop (*"The adolescents should see that we are seekers. And we should direct them toward the path of seekers"* 31, 233 ff.). There must be no blurring or obliteration of the given configurations of age and roles, but the awareness must be present that the potential abilities and life tasks of the young person might well exceed the horizon and possibilities of the teacher. In the lecture cycle "The Younger Generation," Rudolf Steiner said in October 1922:

> It is not our task as teachers to bring the children to the degree of cleverness that corresponds to our own, but to the degree that they are destined to achieve. This means that, as teachers, we might well have to educate someone who exceeds our own abilities. It is obviously impossible to furnish schools with enough teachers if one is not of the opinion that it does not matter that the teacher is not as clever as the pupil will be one day. He will still be able to be a good teacher, because it is not the conveyance of knowledge that counts but the individuality, the bringing to life of the pre-earthly existence. Then children will educate themselves through us. And this is how it should be, because, in reality, we are not educating. We will disturb the education only if we interfere with it too strongly. We educate by behaving in a manner such that through our behavior, children can educate themselves. (217, 163)

Six months later, Steiner said to the teachers in Dornach:

> [...] The best a child can be given during the first and second seven-year period is what awakens by itself with the arrival of puberty, surprising the teacher as it emerges out of the individuality so that the teacher has to say: I have only been a tool in this process. Without this attitude one cannot be a true teacher. After all, the teacher sees the most varied personalities and must not stand in the classroom thinking: the way I am, all the students that I teach must become as well. That must never happen. Why not? Because, if I am lucky, there might be among the students that I have in front of me, apart from the slow ones [...] three or four especially gifted children. And you have to admit that one cannot just employ geniuses as teachers, and that it does happen quite often that a teacher does not have the ingenuity that the students might reach one day. Teachers have to be able to not only educate and teach those students who might be like them one day, but also those who are destined to grow far beyond them. Teachers can, however, only do this if they get rid of the habit of wanting to make a student into what they are themselves. And if they can decide to stand in the classroom, selfless to the extreme, eliminating their own sympathies, antipathies, and personal characteristics, and devote themselves to what the student—unconsciously—says to them, then teachers can educate the genius as well as the slow one. (306, 130 ff.)

In an education for adolescents, the individuality of the young person, which senses and increasingly takes hold of itself, has to experience the necessary conditions of its unfolding on all levels of its incarnating being. In a certain respect, it should be able to actively rely on itself and its own powers, guided, encouraged, supported, and confirmed by the pedagogical theme of the "awakening deed"; that is, supported to realize those (inherent) possibilities and existential destiny-intentions that show themselves in a rudimentary way in concrete ideals and strivings.[44] On April 20, 1923, Rudolf Steiner said in Dornach: *"We have to provide the most favorable environment, so that children can educate themselves through us in the way that they must educate themselves according to their inner destiny"* *(306, 131).*

*

Within the margins of these existential intentions, the young person who has reached puberty reaches out toward a future which, although anticipated to a certain extent initially, has now a more clandestine character. A pedagogy for adolescents that sees as one of its most important tasks the preparation of the young person for what is going to come, will have to do this while considering that the present time which is currently experienced and historically recognized is not identical with this future; in other words, that this pedagogy educates toward an end that is largely unknown.

> In a way, the teacher has to be a prophet. After all, he deals with what will live in the future generation, not in the present. [...]
> This means that in us must live that which only future generations will bring to the surface. We have to cultivate in ourselves a prophetic connection with the future development of humankind. With this close connection stands and falls the pedagogical-artistic feeling, thinking, and willing of a teacher's world. [...]
> That we have to educate in a prophetic way, that we have to anticipate the tasks of the next generation, that is absolutely serious. That is a genuine part of the world. (298, 28 ff.)

Before the first Grade 10 started in the Stuttgart Waldorf School, Steiner again emphatically impressed on the responsible teachers that in order to teach adolescents successfully, they had to grow deeply into the spirit of the time that forms the background for themselves and the young people, but that, at the same time, they had to go beyond it, and into the future. His words are:

> [Teachers] must not hold on to the basic character that lives in the thinking and mentality of people at the present time. [...] We have to grow beyond what time can give us. We must not be puppets of the spirit of our own time [...]. (302, 94/95)
>
> [...] We have to see clearly that what has been educated in us really has to take hold now, has to become an active force; and this can only happen on the basis of a conscience-research that is appropriate for our time, and that goes beyond the individual person. Without this kind of contemporary inner research we cannot grow beyond the perimeter of the present time. (302, 95)

Although Rudolf Steiner's comprehensive but methodically difficult lecture from which the above quotation is taken did not bring to clear expression what he meant by a "contemporary" (or "time-appropriate") "conscience-research" *(Gewissenserforschung),* it still stated distinctly the existential challenge presented by a youth pedagogy and its immanent problems. The entire background of the teachers, all their inner experiences and ways of thinking, carry the signature of their own time-culture, which the young person, in reality, sets out to rise above—departing into an open space, toward social circumstances and challenges, but also toward individual and generational tasks and enterprises that are already immanent in the crises of adolescence, and that not only put into question the teacher's traditional scope of understanding, but threaten to seek to dissolve and overrule it. Doubtlessly, Rudolf Steiner tried to awaken in the responsible teachers of the Stuttgart Waldorf School at least the awareness of this severe tension before the actual high school teaching began: awareness as a starting point for an individual schooling path. In the lecture of June 17, 1921, quoted above, Steiner continues as follows:

> As a matter of fact, humankind always tried to conceal from itself the fact that an extensive conscience-research is needed; something that would thoroughly stir up the inner life with the question: How do we stand here today as adults before the young people? There can only be one answer to this question: if we look at the adolescent boys and girls who are reaching sexual maturity, if they come toward us after this process of maturation, we have to admit if we are really honest: we don't know what to do with them if we don't actively develop an education and teaching methods that are based on entirely new principles. We find ourselves before an abyss that we have created between ourselves and the adolescents. (302, 96)

> It is a matter of summarizing all education and teaching in a basic feeling so that you can, in a way, sense in your soul the powerful impact of this task: we have to place young people right into the world. Without that, our school will be an empty phrase. We will say all sorts of beautiful things about our school, but we will walk on a ground that is full of holes, and eventually, the holes will become so big that there is no ground left to walk on. (302, 94 ff.)

A spiritual-scientific anthropology, however, shows clearly that the ability to anticipate the future pedagogically is intimately related to, even if not entirely identical with, the education of the child's or adolescent's real individuality. What lives and gradually unfolds itself in individual adolescents as a specific anticipation of the future in the present, belongs largely to their individuality, their individual life-intentions in the context of specific generational time-tasks. The growing into and beyond a particular time-configuration, which Steiner expects of teachers, implies therefore what he called the "growing together with the future development of humankind" at the level of a personal, will-carried relationship; it implies no primary insight into or vision of the future on the part of responsible educators, but rather the willingness that they have developed and continue to develop so that they can become, through an inner connection with the adolescents, a selfless organ of perception and assistance. Already in 1905, Rudolf Steiner said:

> What will come to humankind in ten years' time will be known by those human beings who live their lives as individualities. I must not determine the child whom I am educating out of my own self, but I have to obtain out of the child's mysterious inner essence what is entirely unknown to me. (53, 312)

3.

"The teachers completely lost touch with the high school students"

Rudolf Steiner's Criticism of the Teachers at the First Waldorf School

> That I was absent from the school for so long has had negative effects. The teachers completely lost touch with the high school students. [...] If they were incapable! But that is not the case. The problem is that they are lacking enthusiasm; they are lacking active joy in their work. People want to keep doing the same things, they want routine; they want to be a heavy mass rather than an incentive. They are basically inert. (Rudolf Steiner, October 11, 1922; GA 263/1, 103)

FROM THE SUMMER OF 1921 onward, and particularly in the three years until 1924, Rudolf Steiner's faculty meetings with the teachers of the Stuttgart Waldorf School frequently focused on the problems of adolescence and on the contents and structure of the high school, but also on questions about how to meet, guide, and accompany these young people in the right way.[45] Despite his high appreciation for the extraordinary abilities and knowledge of the faculty of the first Waldorf school,[46] and his unbroken trust in them, it cannot be ignored how emphatically he spoke about certain difficulties that occurred at that time and their methodical characteristics. Steiner had, very consciously, given preparatory talks before the foundation of a tenth grade. Whether they were understood in the right way, whether they were internalized and realized, must remain at least debatable. As a matter of fact, Rudolf Steiner urgently pleaded for these lectures to be looked at again: *"I would recommend that you read these four lectures in which I talked about the age of sexual maturity, read those lectures again [...]"* (300c, 75).

During the last years of his presence in the Stuttgart school it became increasingly obvious that Rudolf Steiner, through his own personality, could temporarily mend and partly solve the problems that emerged after the establishment of the high school. In his meetings with the young people, he implemented the pedagogical principles that he had presented in his anthroposophical-anthropological lectures. He obviously also lived within the spirituality of the time, and of that which was to come, and had special access to the growing generations and the individualities that worked in it. On the other hand, he pointed out to the teachers again and again the way in which they could employ the ethics of a youth pedagogy self-reliantly and independently of him.

*

Repeatedly, Rudolf Steiner was asked for advice and support in everyday school situations on how to deal with discipline, by teachers who were often out of their depth (while being closely scrutinized by the public at the same time), and also by the students who were involved in the conflicts. In May 1922, the entire Grade 10 asked to speak to Rudolf Steiner, and described their situation. When Steiner returned for a faculty meeting in October, after new discipline problems had occurred, he said:

> The teachers completely lost touch with the students of the higher grades. This is not something new. It became

quite clear already when the students of the highest grade asked me for a meeting. This fact in itself showed clearly that the contact with the students was lost. This is what lies at the bottom of this situation. As soon as a genuine contact is established, the things that have happened will not happen again. (300b, 138)

Steiner urged the responsible teachers most emphatically not only to solve discipline problems "amicably" (300b, 92), but to take a deep interest in the adolescents in order to come to understand them. Quite frequently, individual students of the school came to him and asked to talk to him if they were having difficulties; among these were also downright outsiders who had gone through difficult socialization processes and traumatic experiences. About a boy who had been considered almost uneducable because of his often antisocial behavior, who had been asked to leave and had later returned (just to be expelled again), Rudolf Steiner said during a meeting with the teachers:

> While this boy was growing up and learning to speak, he never heard a truthful word from his family. The mother is totally untruthful; the father is totally untruthful. They worked against each other, so that the boy came to ask himself one day, when he was about seven or eight years old: How is this world? My father is such a terrible blockhead and they still made him a doctor. How is that possible? Then [the boy] was sent to school and found that the teachers were all blockheads, too. He came to us and said to himself: they say about the Waldorf School that the teachers are not blockheads. I want to see for myself whether they are blockheads or not. Then he was told in so many words that anthroposophy was not being taught here. But anthroposophy was exactly what he wanted. It would have been right for him. He was looking for the opportunity to get to know anthroposophy. He wanted to

know why this was held back. It seemed untruthful to him. He left very soon, worked, and earned some money. After a long time had passed he came to me and said: "I don't know what to do with myself. I had great hopes that they would make a better person of me in the Waldorf School. I went by bike over to Dornach and looked at the Goetheanum. The building always made me a better person. But I can't get anywhere. I see no difference between good and evil. And I don't see why I should become good now. Why should I not become a person who does his best to destroy everything?" (300b, 123 ff.)

When some students had broken the school rules, Steiner tried to get to the bottom of the story by talking with the young people. After he had met with a group of students who, among other things, had disfigured the lavatory doors, he reported the positive outcome of the conversation to the teachers and pointed out in particular the *"dignified human attitude"* of the individual students during their meeting ("I asked them for an example of what they had written on the doors. Their answer was that they could not say that in front of a respectable person. They are also bashful, keen on decorum" 300c, 73/74); and he basically acted as their advocate before the teachers:

> They are actually splendid young people [...]. And as far as self-knowledge is concerned many an adult could learn from them [...]. They are imbued with a certain sense of truthfulness. They are not lacking intelligence. And if one directs their intelligence in the right way, one can without a doubt achieve much. They are really splendid youngsters. I must say that anybody who judges them too severely must have forgotten what it was like to be young [...]. There are many different nuances, but some of them should still be accessible, if one has a good memory. (300c, 73)

And:

> Even if the boys get into the worst mischief, one always has to punish the deed and not the personality. (300c, 83)

*

Several times Rudolf Steiner insisted on keeping a "difficult" adolescent at the school against the wishes of the teachers. He would then describe the problematic biographical background of the individual in question, not in order to induce positive emotional reactions in the teachers or even to achieve disciplinary exceptions, but in order to throw light on the central issues involved in difficult pubertal or adolescent attitudes, and to show methods of dealing with them in a pedagogical way. In the case of a student who had been accused in the faculty meeting of theft and "shamelessly indecent" behavior, Steiner described how the psychological-psychiatric instability of the mother had established itself constitutionally in the son. (*"All that is wrong with this woman psychologically has slipped down from her astral body onto the etheric body of the boy and has become completely organic in him, so that his organic behavior is a true picture of the psychological behavior of the mother. In the mother's astral body it merely comes out as insecurity of judgement, not knowing what to do. In the boy it is that he likes to expose himself."* 300c, 133). He then continued, with advanced pedagogical insights (appealing to the underlying will of the teachers who were sitting in front of him):

> It is, of course, clear to me that, out of sympathy, we have to help this boy reach his eighteenth and nineteenth years. Then his conscience will speak. He first has to properly integrate into his organization the part of his reincarnating "I" that carries his conscience. It is not properly integrated yet, which means that his conscience does not yet

speak at all in situations where in another person it would speak. He is experimenting with all these things, as one always experiments with the higher human being when the lower human being does not incorporate what would hold the personality firmly together. This will take until the eighteenth or nineteenth year. One has to treat him benevolently, otherwise one is responsible for the consequences if he is led to spoil himself, or if what emerges remains spoilt. The boy is so gifted, after all. But his talent does not keep up with his moral constitution. Moral insanity is organically present in him. Now, it is important that out of sympathy one gets such children to grow out of a certain age, but without approving of what they are doing. (300c, 134)

In the end this boy, much to Rudolf Steiner's regret, also had to leave the school because he committed more breaches of discipline. With reference to this and to what he had said four months earlier (see earlier quote), Steiner emphasized during his penultimate faculty meeting in Stuttgart on July 15, 1924:

This boy was mentally slightly deficient and could have been treated with continuous intense psychological therapies. That is why I always said when we talked about him: if we can treat the boy in a way that allows him to develop confidence in a teacher whom he can see as a father figure and to whom he can turn when he needs help, the whole situation could improve. But I have the impression that it was not possible for [the boy] to develop this strong love for a teacher. That could have helped him to improve. In a case like this, instruction does not help, nor do discussions about moral issues. The only thing that helps is a relationship to a teacher to whom the child feels particularly attached. This kind of relationship could not be established. I had hoped for that to be possible. Now he has left. And we cannot say that we did much to strengthen his moral disposition. (300c, 184)

Another "difficult" young man who was repeatedly discussed in the pedagogical conferences had been accepted by the school on Rudolf Steiner's special recommendation a year earlier. When introducing the boy on July 17 and September 18, 1923, he had said:

> I would like to register a student myself [...]. He is sixteen years old and will therefore join the ninth grade. Now this boy is best at philosophy; he knows Plato, Kant, *The Philosophy of Freedom;* he is good at mathematics; weak in Latin, German, and history; mediocre in geography and natural history; and awful at drawing. You have to keep all that in mind. But we cannot put him with the eighth grade. He already completed year 9 in a junior high school. He would also be too old. There is also the matter of finding boarding for him. One has to look into that. [...]
> He is also precocious. He is very gifted and sensible, but one always has to make him work. I warned him that he should show interest in the subjects at school. He has read Plato, Kant, *The Philosophy of Freedom.* He is a bit scattered. If you think that he needs learning support lessons, then he should have them. He would prefer us to analyze *Esoteric Science* for him. He has had several school changes. First he went to a convent school. He will be a hard nut to crack. (300c, 84 ff.)

In this case also, despite the decided warnings, the pedagogical situation took a course which proved unsatisfactory in Rudolf Steiner's view. At the end of the ninth grade, Steiner concluded that the teachers had not at all done justice to the boy and had not shown the *"necessary will to individualize"*; in fact, they had not really met the boy and had acted against the specific intentions of Waldorf education. When Rudolf Steiner saw the report the boy had received, he was horrified and said in the faculty meeting of June 2, 1924:

> The [...] report makes me sad. I made it very clear that it was my decision to take him on—[...] because I thought it necessary that the Waldorf School should not appear rigid. We cannot afford to become rigid, we have to become broad-minded. One cannot run a Waldorf school and rely on finding support if one becomes narrow-minded and rigid. This was a matter of solving a problem in a broad-minded manner, and that is why this boy came to us. I certainly never made a secret of the fact that we were taking on a difficult case. I said it all clearly. We have to look at the question this way. We took on this boy into the ninth grade who was gifted far beyond his years. What kind of questions does he ask? On the other hand, he can't do anything. He is a good-for-nothing in all subjects. Now he was given a report that completely ignores everything that was said before. It was written—and this is enough to drive me up the wall—without regard to this special case; in a routine way, without taking into consideration the boy's psychological state. I have been terribly disgraced by the Waldorf teachers. The report has no meaning for this boy. [...] The report does not convey the fact that the boy spent the most important year of his life here, and that he is a different person now because of it. There is nothing positive in it. He need not have come to a Waldorf school to get this kind of report. (300c, 168 ff.)

In almost all the difficult cases discussed in the faculty meetings, Rudolf Steiner saw that what was missed was the individualizing aspect of the education, the alertness and openness for the future in the attitude of the teachers toward the emerging individuality of the young person, and at the same time their personal interest in him or her. ("*The teachers have not developed a sufficiently deep insight into the psychology of the individual students. That is not a matter of investing a lot of time, but that one develops a fine feeling for this contact so that the students understand rightly what the teacher strives to achieve. This is an ability that one can acquire. What there is now is a certain distance.*" 300c, 187)

The young people were, however, in Rudolf Steiner's view, looking for a genuine relationship with their teachers, although their behavior might have given rise to the opposite impression ("*They want the teachers to know them, to show an interest in them. That is what they want. [...] They want contact with the teacher.*" 300c, 83). Instead, they constantly felt that despite the genuine content that the Waldorf School supplied, they were left to themselves and had lost touch with their educators.[47] From the fifteenth year on, they slipped away from the teachers and went through the difficult years of maturation without the necessary guidance and moral support;[48] a situation that was not helped by the episodic and rather counterproductive efforts of individual teachers to meet the students "on their own level." ("*Then you said to the students that you did not want to speak to them as teachers, but person to person. That is absolutely impossible. You make them big-headed. The students should always have the feeling that one speaks to them as teachers. If you put yourself on the same level with the students, you will bring up brats whom you won't be able to handle. You will place yourselves at their mercy if you say something like that to them. [...] You don't have to point out the opposite to the boys, but you must not try to make them believe that you are their age. That is impossible. The children will necessarily be carried away to a certain big-headedness. [...] You will continuously blur the line that must be there between teacher and student.*" 300b, 132 ff.) Steiner repeatedly expressed his opinion that the teachers were actually lacking the fundamental pedagogical-professional will to build a real and specific relationship, speaking of a "kind of inner laziness" (300b, 225) on the part of those teachers whose teaching style[49] not only indicated the lack of a relationship with the students that was intimate and at the same time left them free, but actually made this relationship impossible. What was needed instead was a genuine personal relationship with the individual adolescent that went beyond the teaching—a personal connection that could form the foundation for a wider pedagogical awareness and purposive guidance. Still, during his second-to-last faculty meeting with the teachers in the middle of July 1924, Rudolf Steiner stressed the absolute necessity for such a new beginning:

> We have to grasp these things in their entire psychological magnitude. We have to seriously consider how to overcome this if we want to keep the Waldorf School alive. For the Waldorf School to continue, it needs the combined good will of everybody; maybe a series of faculty meetings at the beginning of the new school year that deal with just this moral attitude of the school. Otherwise we will not get anywhere. Something is seriously missing here. (300c, 185)

On the occasion of his last visit in Stuttgart just before he became ill, Rudolf Steiner announced a new series of pedagogical courses for the teachers (*"I would like to give lectures in September or in the first week of October about the moral aspect of education and teaching."* 300c, 194) However, these lectures did not take place. Steiner wanted a real new beginning for an as yet insufficiently developed youth education (*"I have to make a new impact."* 300c, 189); a new beginning, especially with regard to the development of a pedagogical relationship and to the moral attitude and responsibility of the educator. Two years earlier he had said the following to the faculty of teachers, with reference to his own lectures on educating adolescents:

> The [...] course was given in order to demonstrate the spirit of the Waldorf School. One would have to look at it again so that the right spirit can enter. We must not become too lax. We really have to bring fire into the teaching. We need enthusiasm. That is certainly what is missing in many cases. That is what we need. Otherwise it can easily happen, especially with an educational method such as this one, which strongly depends on the individuality of the teacher, that we achieve the opposite of what we set out to achieve. (300c, 179)

*

The relevance of what Rudolf Steiner had developed in his detailed principles of an anthropology and pedagogy for adolescence became obvious in the continuous problematic, and at times even tragic, destinies of individual young people that we find described in the faculty meetings. The "difficult youngsters" of the Stuttgart Waldorf School were therefore not foremost an extracurricular, psychiatric, or forensic topic, but rather practical examples of what Rudolf Steiner meant by the necessity of a "deepening of the heart" (310, 37 ff.) of the teacher, or by the "inner aspect of the relationship between teacher and adolescent." It is a well-known fact that should be considered in this context that, apart from this, Steiner thought the presence of a school doctor in the faculty of teachers[50] and a learning support class in the school to be essential, and that this was put into practice.[51] It can, nevertheless, not be ignored that the whole issue of support and guidance during puberty and adolescence, as well as the task of pedagogically enabling the adolescent to become socially competent, became particularly apparent in the problems that Rudolf Steiner addressed in such a special and radical way, and with such intensity. This is the reason why he discussed them in the faculty meetings in front of the entire teaching staff.[52] The Waldorf School therefore remained for Rudolf Steiner "a problem child" right to the end. Yet, at the same time, due to its future-orientated intention, which is immensely appropriate for our times and based on real insights, it is *"a landmark for the fruitfulness of anthroposophy in the spiritual life of humankind"* (Letter to the faculty of teachers, March 15, 1925; 260a, 405).

Addenda

Rudolf Grosse
"Your teachers think day and night about what your future will be like"

Rudolf Steiner and the First Graduates of the Stuttgart Waldorf School, 1924

Eugen Kolisko
"The present world situation"

Speech Given at a Reunion of Former Waldorf Students Stuttgart, October 13, 1930

Ita Wegman
"We fight for each soul"

Letter to Ernst Lehrs Concerning the Education of Adolescents, January 20, 1931

Rudolf Grosse

"Your teachers think day and night about what your future will be like"

Rudolf Steiner and the First Graduates of the Stuttgart Waldorf School, 1924[53]

AFTER OUR GRADUATION, our class asked Rudolf Steiner for advice about what professions and trainings we might choose. Some time later he said that it was not easy to advise a Waldorf student on this because Waldorf schooling would have awakened such a wide range of interests that he could see many possibilities.

We gathered on April 10, 1924, filled with the highest expectation in the teachers' room, for this requested meeting. Seventeen students, eight girls and nine boys, sat around the big table that took up most of the room, while our teachers were sitting along the walls. A kind of feeling took hold of us all, as one experiences before making important life decisions, and all eyes were directed toward Rudolf Steiner who had taken his seat at the head of the table. It was very quiet when he addressed us in his calm, full voice. As we had asked for this gathering, he said, we should now say what we had in mind, and it would best if we spoke one after the other. He asked the girl closest to him to begin. We now listened with amazement to the intimate dialogue that developed between each pupil and Rudolf Steiner—very factual, almost sober, with a hint of humor here and there.

The advice had a clarifying and directive effect. The students first spoke about their future plans. Rudolf Steiner listened and then gave his advice, which could also be critical. When one girl spoke with great sensitivity about her intention to study psychiatry, he advised strongly against it. Psychiatry, he said, had not advanced enough yet to understand the so-called mental illnesses, and was therefore unable to develop an appropriate method of therapy. For the time being nothing much could be done about that. She should devote herself to the sciences and study physics, chemistry, and philosophy in order to become a teacher of these subjects.

He gave the same advice about studying sciences to another girl. Yet another wanted to become a kindergarten teacher and asked how to go about it. A single sentence illuminated the essence of this profession. It was important that one was loved by the children; everything else would then fall into place. He said it was similar for a nurse whose healing quality lay in the fact that she had to be a personality whom the patients could trust. She had to be strong enough to bear the egotism of sick people, and to never weary of doing her duty. When a girl announced her intention to devote her life to the arts, to painting and carving, he strongly supported her. And, after her training, she should go on as an artist at the new Goetheanum in Dornach. Some received very short indications, for example two boys, where one was told to embark on a business career and to become a craftsman. The other boy wanted to become an architect. To my astonishment, he quietly advised against it and tried to interest him in mechanical engineering. What are missing today, he said, are aesthetically constructed machines. The design of an engine was entirely determined by its function without any consideration for beauty. Central Europe in particular should take hold of this impulse. It did not come from the West, but the West could then learn from it. It did matter what a machine such as a train engine looked like. It had to be beautiful. One should learn to pay attention to this and work also out of a sense of beauty when designing an engine. [...]

Rudolf Steiner, who was now standing, concluded this mentoring session—which for other students was confined to questions about their further education and examinations, and would become more concrete in a meeting half-a-year later—with the following words: "You are leaving school now, but we will meet again in half a year. Each of you can then report how you got on during this time. The memory of your school will accompany you into the life that lies ahead of you, and if, in later life, you come to a point where you are at a loss, at your wits' end and alone, pondering and searching for help, the spirit of the school will stand behind you, put a hand on your shoulder, and bestow advice and comfort to you. You have asked for a verse and I have written it down here." He read the verse slowly, and we received it with the highest inner concentration. He said we should take this verse into our hearts and meditate on it. He then bid us farewell and we left the room, happy and reassured, because we would always be able to meet and consult with him. I felt a deep inner confidence because of his guidance that was quite palpable. [...]

This important mentoring moment with Rudolf Steiner had been preceded by one of his great lectures, which he had given at the end of the school year, on March 27, 1924. We high school students who were about to leave the Waldorf School in order to go to universities, into professional training, or straight into practical work, were full of questions about the future. We also experienced a subtle wrench, because this was the last time that we were, in this familiar way, part of what had become our spiritual home of genuine human education. Rudolf Steiner's parting words were like a gift that would last forever. The following sentences are forever engraved in my memory: "Your teachers think day and night about what your future will be like. I can tell you that in ten or twenty years' time, the situation will be much worse than the terrible years we went through and that we are experiencing now. A deep sorrow darkens the soul when one thinks of the great suffering that this future holds for humankind. The teachers are also sad to dismiss you now from this school, but it will be a source of great strength for them to see you all prove yourselves as true human beings."[54] These were basically his words. Deep in thought, I went home after this assembly, working out again and again in my mind: Now it's the year 1924; in ten years it will be 1934 and in twenty years 1944. I will be between 30 and 40 then, and will have to live through a historical age that will be more terrible than anything I experienced before. [...]

On the first of September the entire former class gathered again at the Waldorf School. Rudolf Steiner had not returned yet from England. We decided to write him a letter to let him know that we were waiting for him, as agreed; that we wanted to tell him what we had experienced so far and ask his further advice for the situations that had unfolded. These were our words:

Waldorf School, September 1, 1924

> Dear Dr. Steiner,
> When we had the privilege of meeting with you at the end of our time in the Waldorf School, you suggested that we should come together again once we had gone out into the world. This has happened now and almost the entire former class 12 is here in Stuttgart, hoping to be able to speak with you and our teachers again. The experiences we have had in the meantime urge us to come here.
> With grateful respect
> Class 12

The conference on the next day, when we met Dr. Steiner and Dr. Wegman, was in our view the beginning of a series of such meetings. Rudolf Steiner himself put it like this: *"From now on, come every year at this time to the school and share with your teachers what you have experienced in your lives. The teachers will then give you lectures on what they have researched in the meantime. In this way, a kind of school for further education in the spirit of the Waldorf School will be established."* The reports that several of us now gave of our experiences seemed to be of the greatest interest to Rudolf Steiner. Especially when one student spoke about his life as a student working in a factory, about his relationship with the workers, their initial distrust and reticence which gradually disappeared and made way for open conversations. Steiner said that Waldorf students in particular should try to make this kind of contact, but that one had to always speak truthfully with the workers. That needed time, patience, and ever-new attempts.

Following similar reports, he said about medical studies that one should not ignore these areas, because they were spiritually not what they ought to be; and that the same was true for technology. Then: nursing is a difficult profession, because the nurse is dealing with people who are often totally moody and egotistic in soul and spirit. The essence of this profession is a kind of sacrificial service that one should see as inner development. A good nurse, just as a kindergarten teacher, should not know why she loves the patients or the children. The atmosphere that emanates from her is important. These comments were similar to the ones we had heard during our first meeting.

He gave further advice to the student who wanted to go into business. Here it was important to acquire thorough practical experience, and to develop, presence of mind. One should know the usages of world trade, which could be studied in their purest form in England or America. They were quite distasteful, but instructive. One could learn a lot for the development of the economic life of Central Europe from studying the practices and affairs that had become established among the great trading nations; not so that one could copy them, but so that one would be able to see through them.

Many other things were commented on; for example, the general pedagogical interest of adolescents at the time. It was important to refer to education as an art. It was no science, and as soon as one developed it as a system it was immediately a sign of decadence, because such an education no longer knew what to do with adolescents.

At the end he reminded us again of the verse he had given to us, and asked us to work with it more intensely than before:

May those things shine again
On the path through life
That in the time of youth
Were planted in the heart
As the seal of true humanity.

May those things be strong
In the depth of memory
Which the soul discovered
Through the heart
Under the spirit guidance
Of the powers that teach for life.

Rudolf Steiner's verse for the graduates
of the Stuttgart Waldorf School,
April 1924 (GA 40, p. 356)

Eugen Kolisko

"The present world situation"

Speech Given at a Reunion of Former Waldorf Students Stuttgart, October 13, 1930[55]

DEAR FRIENDS,

Some of you have asked me to speak about the present world situation. This is so because we believe that our reunions also have the purpose of forming a picture of what is going on in the world today—of the big questions that move the present age. This meeting is special also because we can look back over seven years of coming together as a community.

In our reunions, we want to try to connect what moves us here as a community to the great events of life. We can only give basic indications today concerning the spiritual background of the world situation and what part of it can move us, take hold of us and interest us, and what tasks it holds for us; but still, such indications must not be missing from our gathering.

What mainly characterizes the present time is that there never was an era when humanity was as helpless as it is today in the face of its own amazing creations, in the face of what it has brought about in terms of cultural progress and transformation, its great inventions, and its organization of the whole world. More than ever, it is faced with its creations, with the modern worldview and the modern culture that it has created out of freedom; and the fact is that it cannot control the consequences.

On the one hand, we have our ideal of the human being which unites us, and on the other hand, the human being is faced with overwhelming achievements of our time. This manifests on different levels. One could mention the enormous changes in our civilization over the last decades, which have exceeded anything that happened during the whole of the nineteenth century. We get the impression when we look at all the inventions and discoveries—for example, at the transformation of our environment by the use of electricity—that all these inventions bring the nations closer together. Radio, film, and television connect people all over the world so that today we can speak of a global connection among human beings. And this development moves on with giant steps. The world seems to get smaller and smaller, and barriers are overcome. Distances become shorter, and it does not seem extraordinary anymore when someone travels through Europe from London to Rome—something that used to be very special indeed. One would think that such a time requires an enormous inner development, through which human beings can become worthy of being world citizens of today. Mr. Boy[56] spoke about what connects all of us. Perhaps it is that we have a shared ideal of the human being, which we all absorbed because Rudolf Steiner worked here and was a living example for us. Many of you experienced this personally. With Waldorf education, he wanted to give something that would lead toward this ideal.

There is something particular about these great inventions and discoveries, and one can observe this increasingly: We are discovering more and more ways of sending messages all over the world by using electricity—and maybe we will soon be able to see people to whom we are speaking on the telephone. We discover more and more ways of bringing people together. This is possible because we have surrounded the earth with a network of electricity, of electrical currents.

What we don't have today is a science that looks at the divine. We don't know what electricity in the earth's atmosphere and all these inventions will do to human beings. We have no science that can keep up with them. How does being surrounded by electricity affect people's health? We see the same in other areas. New inventions are constantly being made because science has moved on tremendously since the beginning of the twentieth century.

Before, the new things invented by science were still able to be mastered and controlled. The new substances that were being discovered could be controlled by the scientists. Then they discovered radiation in all chemical substances, such as x-rays, for example. Today, one knows that every living thing gives off radiation. There is no substance left of which the chemical composition is unknown. We have reached a point now that is new in the field of science; we have moved on from things that are tangible and contained to those that spread everywhere, that radiate out into the entire space, into the etheric.

The whole field of electricity, the invention of the radio—they are all connected with this; they take us into the world of substances that one can't see next to oneself, but that radiate out into space. And today all these radiations are immediately put to use; for example, to influence and improve food quality. People don't know anymore what they are working with, such as in the case of ultraviolet radiation. Things are discovered and quickly promoted as good and healthy; then, some professor finds out that they are bad, that they are the worst poison. Long discussions ensue, and then the wonder-cure disappears. In the meantime, two to four new ones have been found, and the process repeats itself. Looking back over this development, one finds that scientists can no longer keep up; they do not understand how the things work that they have released into the world.

Let us look at the use of electricity as a fertilizer. Electrical wires have been put up over vast areas of America to generate a strong electrical effect. As a consequence, agricultural products can be mass produced. There are certain rays, infrared rays, which one cannot see but which have a warming effect. They enhance germination to the extent that one can achieve two harvests. This will, no doubt, be brilliantly developed in no time. Soon we will no longer be able to eat natural products because everything has been treated in one way or another. There are companies in America that scatter arsenic and lead salts—Persil—over their vast orchards. This works as a pesticide. Then, one reads in a scientific magazine that a chemist has found out that the skin and outer part of the apples form an indissoluble chemical compound with the arsenic, but only the experts know this.

Now one asks oneself: What does it do, if it cannot be washed off? Maybe soon there won't be any alternative types of apples? I could give you thousands of similar examples.

It is remarkable that human beings keep on making discoveries that can no longer be controlled. It was different at the time of the steam engine; science only went as far as its discoveries. There was a time when physicians had fully explored the human body, diseases, and where they come from. Only one thing remained difficult: how to cure them. In the 1860s or 70s there was even a medical school with prominent scientists who thought that one could just as well give patients sugar, as long as they believed that they were being cured. This was a serious view, supported by eminent researchers. As far as healing was concerned, there were not so many discoveries. That has changed since the discovery of x-rays. Since then it has become something of an obsession; everything that is discovered has to be put into practice. But one does not know how it works. There are other things that once were not possible. It was discovered that nitrogen is the main component of air. It stays at the top; it is inert and not easily moved. Those of you who know something about chemistry will remember that with the help of electricity, one can fix the nitrogen and convert it into saltpetre, which is the main component of gunpowder. People used to be able to do this only on a small scale, until the time came when someone found out about fixing the nitrogen. Since then, nitrogen has been used to produce explosives all over the world. There must be enough today to blow up half the earth. What was not possible before, now makes a difference to the world as a whole.

Humankind learned to gain something from pure air with which one could now, if one were so inclined, blow up half the earth. It was not the case before that technical achievements had the potential to become natural disasters. In the past, the greatest disasters were accidents, now they are caused by civilization.

Then, toxic gases were developed—war gases—and more and more ways of producing them. This has to do with technology. It is known today that all businesses producing artificial silk could be converted into war industries any time. One turn of the lever and something that is useful becomes destructive.

I wanted to mention these things because they are characteristic of our times. We cannot look at today's world situation without realizing that with the discoveries and inventions that have been made, it depends entirely on human beings whether they are employed to build something or to destroy half the world. This is true not only for the substances I mentioned, but also for the human being's soul life. It would not have been possible in the past to invent something like the cinema, which has conquered the whole world. It is really interesting how it has spread from its first beginnings. It has had an unbelievable impact. Nobody intended or imagined that it would suddenly be possible that the works of our writers would be turned into films and that the theater would be ruined by it. Schiller called the theater a place for moral education. It is different today. [...]

Today, cinema has usurped almost the entire art world, and one cannot even say that this was intended. The effect cinema has on education is not exactly positive. Not long ago, a film was made about Jesus Christ. A section of the English army filmed it in Palestine with the pope's permission. People actually dared to do this and take part in it. Just imagine what the

English army did there: such a blasphemy about events that were of central importance for humanity. They just did it there. Nobody asks how this came about. Nobody asks what was necessary to produce such a film; what was needed was that a sensible human being not undertake Christ's life as fiction! Nobody in their right mind would think of producing something like that.

I want to show how cinema has a power we cannot elude. Cultural phenomena never used to spread in the way cinema does. They used to spread through human consciousness. We have now entered a completely new era. The last ten years have shown that this process, which has to be met by a new culture, is on the increase. Humanity can no longer control the consequences of its inventions, for example, the inventions based on electricity. The only way to control them would be by intensely developing spiritual life through thinking. But before this can happen, the general outlook has to be extended to include the spiritual life.

It is the same in the field of economics. There used to be famines and all sorts of problems that were due to deprivation. But it never happened in the history of humankind that diseases developed out of opulence to an extent that affected the overall economy. This symptom arose where modern scientific theories were put into practice and were eagerly spread all over the world. This has to do with America taking on a leading role. In 1898, there was a war between Spain and America. Hardly any wars seem as ludicrous as this one. Most people were convinced that Spain would win. Spain was the great empire of Philipp II, an empire in which the sun never set. This empire rose against America. It seems ludicrous today. Now the strange thing happened that the British Empire also subordinated itself to America. It is staggering that a British prime minister travels to New York to negotiate financial issues between the British Empire and America. This is more a political point, but what I am trying to get at is that America is taking on a leading role. European civilization, which used to be dominant, comes from the West, is taken up by America and spread all over the world. Many things were developed in Germany, but it is via America that they reach the rest of the world. There used to be plenty of bakers in Europe, for example, but an abundant supply of sugar could only be produced once big plantations appeared. A way of using the waste product of this to make liqueur was also discovered. It was like that with many things that came from the West. It is remarkable how things move on, and then come back with increased speed and spread all over the world. It is because of modern economies that it is possible to change the whole world so that technological processes overtake cultural processes; this is possible in America.

Electricity is a natural power. When it enters the natural process, it spreads like an avalanche, and the human spirit and soul cannot cope with it. It is typical that small things can evolve into enormous and world-embracing processes. We cannot stop these natural effects; there is no way to do that. The question is rather: how can human beings change fast enough to keep up with them? Technology is nature today; it is just there. The difference between nature and technology has become blurred. Telegraph wires span the Earth. Now the phenomena of the atmosphere and the climate are being investigated with a view to influencing the weather. We are moving toward a complete change of the conditions of the world. This goes hand in hand with the changes in technology and engineering.

Whereas this progress happens on the one side, voices have become louder in the East over the last ten or twenty years that say that European civilization is worthless, that it is destructive and that it kills human beings. These voices are particularly strong in the areas where there are still the ancient cultures: in India, China, and Japan. An increasing sense of moral indignation comes toward us from there. The political phenomena that we witness are a consequence of this. One can see this contrast for example in the fact that Mohandas Gandhi stood up against England. If you have a sense for what is symptomatic in world history you will understand this process. Gandhi opposed the British salt monopoly by organizing a march to the sea where he invited his followers to make their own salt. For those in the ancient East, salt is the shaped, crystal-clear ideal to which the human being rises through self-development. Clear thinking was an ideal to them, something that had religious spiritual significance. On the other side was this economic power that wanted to take possession of the salt. Gandhi opposed this with a spiritual demonstration. There was a struggle between violence and non-violence. This is only to illuminate the contrast between the great Eastern and Western cultures. There are other examples that show this inner indignation about what has become Western civilization.

It is interesting that whole nations, peoples who have older cultures and do not belong to the white race, look at the European-American civilization and ask this big question to those who brought Christianity along with Western culture: How can Europeans and Americans reconcile their Christianity with what happened with opium in China? These double standards don't seem to make sense. A huge crisis has unfolded over the last ten years. Missionaries are no longer convincing with their religion, in the face of what else is coming from the West.

The travelling writer Colin Ross says, interestingly, that we are facing all of these other nations who are asking: What have you done to Christianity! How can it be reconciled? This lives as a real question today not just in the East but everywhere: that this Western European civilization purports to be Christian. But there is a great contradiction in the world with a spiritual-moral structure, on the one hand, and on the other hand, modern rationality that has developed a technology with which it would be possible to launch into the most horrible wars at any time. The entire East and the ancient peoples ask what this is that spreads like an explosion, and that seems to rise up from the earth, wanting to subject it to its influence. These old civilizations are connected with the heavens, whereas the American-European civilization is earthbound. It is as if the heavens were asking: What did you do to Christianity? In contrast to this we have in the middle, in Europe and America, such great human conflicts. And while there is this connection on one side, the spirit stirs on the other and asks the question: what has become of me?

What characterizes the modern world situation is that a mediating element is missing that could balance out this contrast. Americanism is penetrating into the East, and the British Empire is the victim. The peoples of the East rise up against it and flee to the West, where it comes to a backlash that grows dangerously out of proportion. Austria used to be seen as the sick old man of Europe; now it is Britain. There is something else. Especially here in Central Europe, one notices how the feeling about things that have been achieved in Europe is disappearing fast. In the French Revolution, people fought for human rights, for the freedom of the individual. The French Revolution passed; the human rights stayed. Later it became freedom of the spirit, and it was called Humanism. The human being was put in the center. What is characteristic for Goethe's time is unthinkable without the French Revolution. There was an ideal of the human being to strive toward. What goes together with freedom in spiritual life is today regressing in many parts of the world.

Look at the nineteenth century and the great Italian Giuseppe Garibaldi—how he fought the state, and especially the church, and tried to free Italy. He had many enthusiastic followers, also in Europe. Then a boat arrived from the United States and took him along to America.... After a while he returned to Italy. There were people who sympathized with such a personality.

There is no freedom there now; Mussolini destroyed everything that Garibaldi had achieved. Some people would have been up in arms if somebody had been executed for demanding freedom of opinion. That would not happen today, because there is a certain lack of freedom. One can no longer speak of freedom of the spirit in Italy. People are not allowed to say what they think, and the state will not employ anybody who does not share its ideology. It is not like that just in Italy, but also in other places. One has the impression that the human freedom that had been achieved is disappearing. Mussolini says that human rights make people stupid, that one should get rid of them. It was also he who said that human rights are something beautiful, but that cannons are better. This kind of thinking is spreading, not just in the South. Looking at some of the views today, one could think that we are back in the times of the Enlightenment, if not even the Reformation. What is needed is a mediating element. People in Central Europe have forgotten the ground from which great things grew in Germany. Think of the following quite significant symptom: the Goethe Prize was awarded to Professor Freud, the founder of psychoanalysis in Vienna, one of the most famous people in the world. He tried to analyze the unconscious soul. There are not many things that have less to do with the Goethe Prize. [...] This is typical. To whom do they give the Goethe Prize? To the most famous. But you will not find any inner connection between Goethe and Freud. This does not make sense.

There is, for example, a pedagogical debate about whether schools should be governed by the state or by the church. They should not be governed by either of them. Germany was always seen as a country with new ideas on education. But now there is this argument about whether schools should be governed by church or state. This is outdated, because neither church nor state can cope with schools. I just want to point out how little of what happens in German or Central European public life is satisfactory for the people. What should be coming from here is a renewal of the spiritual life, new spiritual ideas. The important question is not whether the church or state should be in charge, but what the German people think. When Germans speculate and lose, it is insignificant. But whether Germans think in the right or wrong way has an impact on the world situation. People relied on Central Europe to produce new ideas about education. Rudolf Steiner developed these and put them into practice in the Waldorf School. Conventional education still follows Greek and Roman traditions—ancient educational approaches that are not suitable for our times. There used to be enormous opposition against the introduction of secondary schools with a practical orientation (*Realschule*). The schools were established, but opposition still continues. The Waldorf School is not an experimental school system; it is the seed for a whole new approach to education. It offers education right up through the high school level. The possibility of a new educational approach is there, but people don't believe in it if they don't see it established. The future is possible, but education has to change. And the seed is there, however imperfect it might still be, as Mr. Boy pointed out in his earlier speech. The relevant question is not how perfect or imperfect it is, but whether we are able to connect to the source. The idea for a new education is there.

The right path can be found today only through a renewal of the entire spiritual life. Only a renewal embracing all of humanity as all processes do today in education, the arts and religion, only knowledge of the spiritual world and the transformation of human consciousness, can solve the conflicts in such a way that humankind can move forward. The separation from history that we have been taught to believe, does not exist in reality. Christianity *is* still as it has developed, and it is up to us to decide whether we want to see the world situation as an expression of only destructive forces. We find ourselves in a terrible world situation, but there are profound spiritual powers of renewal that can embrace the arts, the sciences, and religion in what Rudolf Steiner has given us as Anthroposophy—from which the impulse for a new education also streams forth. Humanity can be united in such a thought—and with this I would like to conclude my contemplation of the world situation. The answer to the great world questions can arise out of such a renewal of the way we look at the world as was brought to us by Rudolf

Steiner. This is not restricted to anthroposophists, it is open to everybody, and everybody can feel connected to it. It is similar with other things. There are so many discussions about agriculture today, how to treat the soil, and so forth. Where can new views come from? Not only the Earth is active, the entire cosmos is. We need a new science that takes into account that the whole cosmos is active, not just the Earth. We need to see this! Agriculture has forgotten about the cosmos. Certain things are already there, and they are developing today in Central Europe. The question is: How one can bridge the huge gap between East and West? Who can solve the big questions of the world and humanity, where European-American civilization stands against the old cultures? This is a big problem. How can science and Christianity be united? That is the most important task of our times. The nineteenth century revealed the contrast between belief and knowledge, but the twentieth century does not know what to do with it, because people think they know it all already. In the nineteenth century, there were people who had religion to support their inner life. How many people are left today who find support in religion? In Goethe's time, people found inner strength through art. Art is no longer seen as something that can shape culture. Contemporary art is struggling to hold its ground. It is the same with science. Since the beginning of the twentieth century, an increasing number of voices have called for science to become religion; now they are regressing. Science does not yet touch the innermost needs of our souls. Today, one could say that human beings believe in a renewal that comes out of the spirit, and that can only be achieved if one takes hold of those powers that stream into the different areas of life. This could go out from Central Europe. It is part of our world situation, and future generations will find this difficult to understand: that it is possible for somebody like Rudolf Steiner to remain unknown. The next conflict can only be solved out of a higher knowledge. At the moment, we see only the outer layer, not the full spiritual reality.

The human ideal that Rudolf Steiner demonstrated in his life and work can only grow if it is carried into of all the different fields of life. Even if we have the impression that we only make a weak contribution toward this transformation, we are still working against the one-sided forces of destruction on a path that leads to the resurrection of the spirit in human evolution.

Ita Wegman

"We fight for each soul"

Letter to Ernst Lehrs Concerning the Education of Adolescents[57]

Arlesheim, January 20, 1931

DEAR DR. LEHRS!

I would like to discuss several things with you. I have been thinking about education a lot recently. I suppose this is because of the children we have here at the *Sonnenhof* [home for children, adolescents, and adults with special needs in Arlesheim/Switzerland, tr.], because of the nurses' training where we also have educational tasks, and also because I occasionally have the opportunity to observe the children in the Waldorf School and in other schools and to have a chat with them. I have discovered that the children think differently now, and are interested in completely different things than the children of five or seven years ago. There is one sentence in Rudolf Steiner's work on education that is very important for me. It says that education must orientate itself by what the teacher finds in the souls of the children in the times they live in. One sees in these children's souls—this is the case mainly in Germany—a tremendous interest in social problems, in political problems, in everything national and international. Children of fourteen or fifteen join communist or national socialist organizations. I heard this not only from children who attend mainstream schools, but also from Waldorf pupils. To my greatest astonishment I read some days ago in a magazine that was sent to me from Berlin, *Die Brücke*, how fourteen- and fifteen-year-old children from different schools write in this magazine what they think about the political life, and what they would like to hear about these things in school. One can see that they have a longing for the right kind of guidance. Then I thought again of Rudolf Steiner's education and of the following sentence: "Education has to follow whatever lives in the hearts of the children." This means that Rudolf Steiner's education, if it strives to be alive, has to be flexible and adjust to the children it wants to educate. And the question arose in me: Would it not be possible to offer these children, these searching souls in the Waldorf Schools—one surely finds them there more than anywhere else, because Rudolf Steiner's form of education awakens more interest than others, so that the pupils develop an open mind toward everything—to offer these children something that can support them in their search for social solutions? And I wondered whether a generously devised course with free discussion about the three-fold social organism for fourteen- or fifteen-year-olds, but with a teacher, with whom they can speak openly; I wondered whether that was not one of the tasks, dear Dr. Lehrs, which the Free Society, and especially you, should take on. I have the feeling that we do not fulfil our tasks as anthroposophists if, when around us we see the needs of human souls, and the needs of the children's souls in particular—which are snatched up by all sorts of organizations that shape their young brains according to their maxims, so that later on there is no way of getting rid of what has been instilled in these children at this age—we fail to realize what Rudolf Steiner wanted: to have schools where children are educated in the right way, so that they become truly human. And this does not really happen, because the Waldorf children are as exposed to the dangers of today's culture as are other children. One could, of course, argue that the children experience so many positive influences at school that the negative ones don't have the same impact on them as they have on other children. Maybe these influences are balanced out safely, but we must not forget that young people are looking for really great tasks, for exciting work, for great aims; and that they are attracted to the sensational and easily enthused, and led one way or another by politics. I could see it as a healing influence if one founded a league for young people, who would take up the ideas of threefoldness with enthusiasm; and if one offered courses and discussions and all sorts of things for these children—also courses for social problems, and so forth. I feel strongly that this is what Dr. Steiner had intended to be the work of the Youth Section, although at the time he was more concerned with upper school students and the graduates. I had the impression when I thought about education that, if we are not vigilant, Rudolf Steiner's education might become stagnant, and thus not remain flexible enough to adjust to the changing times in a way that will be extremely important for these children and their development.

Dear Dr. Lehrs, I don't want to say any more, I just want to share my concerns with you and draw attention to the fact that we have to be careful that we don't gradually lose the young people, those who used to attend the Waldorf School or those who are still going to the Waldorf School. We fight for each soul. We have to think of this, and the teachers have a great responsibility toward these souls. Maybe there will be an opportunity for us to talk about these questions.

I hope you don't take it amiss that I wrote you this letter. All I meant to say is that I would like to hear what you think about this and what your experiences are.

Yours sincerely,
Dr. I. Wegman

Notes

[References from the works of Rudolf Steiner given throughout the text and in the following notes refer to the pages of the German editions (GA). Passages have been newly translated to give consistency of terminology.]

1. References to passages from the works of Rudolf Steiner correspond to the volume number in the Collected Works in German [GA], followed by the page number in the German edition (e.g., 223, 127), except when known in the English edition (e.g., 25 Engl.). See the list of GA volumes starting on p. 121. *(A. Meuss translator of the notes only)*
2. Caroline von Heydebrand (ed.): *Rudolf Steiner in der Waldorfschule*. Stuttgart 1927, p. 52.
3. The crisis—understood as "decision at a stage when new and old are at odds" (Jacob and Wilhelm Grimm: *Deutsches Wörterbuch*. Leipzig 1873, Volume 5, column 2332)—is immanent to the structure of adolescence. If the dissolution and re-formation of vital structures of existence (and incarnation) and the break-up and transformation of the established in favor of new, yet intrinsically jeopardized degrees of freedom are part of the crisis as a phenomenon of the temporality of human existence, then any closer study of adolescence illustrates the suitability of this term for the inevitable imbalance that goes with it (see below).
4. Rudolf Steiner's unique spiritual presence in the first Waldorf School in Stuttgart, and his whole relationship to the school that he directed, need urgent and comprehensive reassessment. This would, in my view, be essential for the future of the Waldorf movement. Apart from Karl Schubert's minutes of the faculty meetings, Steiner's lectures and lecture

cycles on education (and on anthroposophy in general), and the numerous documents of the Rudolf Steiner Archives, such a monograph should also take into account Caroline von Heydebrand's memories of the teaching faculty (see Note 2), and various recollections of the high school students themselves (see below).

5   Erhard Fucke: *Grundlinien einer Pädagogik des Jugendalters. Zur Lehrplankonzeption der Klassen 6 bis 10 an Waldorfschulen.* [Basic principles of an education for adolescence. The Waldorf curriculum for classes 6 to 10] Stuttgart 1991.

6   Karl-Martin Dietz: *Erziehung in Freiheit. Rudolf Steiner über Selbständigkeit im Jugendalter.* [Education in Freedom. Rudolf Steiner on self-reliance in adolescence] Heidelberg 2003.

6a Ibid., page 8.

7   Fucke, loc. cit., p. 212, writes in his epilogue with regard to this: "On the occasion of the Waldorf School celebrating its 70th anniversary there was many a review. Understandably, these concentrated primarily on the successes of the Waldorf movement and the many ideas that the state school system could take from it. This is justified. This book also celebrates the great inspirations that Waldorf education is able to give to general educational approaches. —The author believes, however, that he has to do justice to Rudolf Steiner's intention also by drawing attention here and there to those of his aims that have not been achieved yet. One has to be clear about the fact that Rudolf Steiner had to work with premises that could not be easily changed: the teachers, school legislation, circumstances, etc. —Those who, like me, met some of the teachers who used to work under Rudolf Steiner, look back with great fondness to these encounters; not least because they opened our eyes to the atmosphere that prevailed at the time of the foundation of the first Waldorf School, and because they had such an essential influence on our personal development. It nevertheless becomes obvious—for example, when one reads through the faculty

meetings—that some teachers did not really understand Rudolf Steiner in certain situations, and went as far as ignoring or obstructing his intentions. Such intentions can only become socially effective if they are received in the right way. This means that the creator of Waldorf education depends on the powers of comprehension of those in charge of putting the intentions into practice." (Ibid., p. 211)

8   Cf. e.g. Iwan, Rüdiger: *Ansätze zur Entwicklung einer neuen Oberstufengestalt.* [Proposals for the development of a new high school structure] Stuttgart 2003; *Phantasie und Verantwortung. Projektunterricht als Anliegen der Waldorfpädagogik.* [Imagination and responsibility. The role of project work in Waldorf education] Heidelberg 2004.

9   Concerning "maturity of the senses," "maturity of breathing," and "maturity for earth" see Rudolf Steiner's curative education course [GA 317], lecture of June 25, 1924. His physiology of development and the formulations used in the lecture suggest that all three systems of physiological function are fully developed or "mature" only when the child is "mature for earth." This stage thus implies maturity gained at the three levels of physiological activity: in the senses (neurosensory system), breathing (rhythmical system), and sexuality (metabolism and limbs). ("We should therefore speak of 'maturity for earth' rather than 'sexual maturity,' and under 'maturity for earth' include maturity in the senses and maturity of breathing, with sexual maturity as another such subdivision." 317, 25 Engl.) We also need to consider that the three systems are in fact developed in the downward incarnating movement, with relative maturity in the senses and breathing gained in the first or second seven-year period (concerning the development of the rhythmical system in the second seven-year period, see, for instance, the detailed information given by Steiner in Selg, P. *Vom Logos menschlicher Physis.* Dornach 2000, p. 613 ff.). The extent to which a qualitative further development of the individual functional organizations still follows in youth, Steiner suggested not only by speaking of processes in which the heart organism is

transformed as part of the rhythmical system (see Note 22), but by saying that will-activity can only penetrate and partly determine the periphery of human senses once sexual maturity is reached. (He spoke of it as one precondition for the adult capacity of sensory and intellectual reference to the world; see GA 218, lecture of November 19, 1922, in London; also Note 29).

10 "Fundamentally, imitation means nothing other than that something is living on, which existed in a totally different form in the spiritual world before birth or conception, where one spirit would enter wholly into another; this then comes to expression in the way children imitate their human environment as an echo of their life in the spirit" (200, 115).

11 Concerning Rudolf Steiner's concept of the neurosensory system, see Selg, P. *Vom Logos menschlicher Physis*, p. 428 ff., and Selg, P. (ed.) *Rudolf Steiner – Quellentexte fuer die Wissenschaften*. Band 3. *Physiologische Menschenkunde* Dornach 2004, p. 247 ff.

12 See relevant passages by Rudolf Steiner in Selg, P. *Vom Logos menschlicher Physis*, p. 593 ff., and in Selg, P. (ed.) *Rudolf Steiner – Quellentexte fuer die Wissenschaften*. Band 3. *Physiologische Menschenkunde*, p. 155 ff.

13 Concerning Rudolf Steiner's concept of the rhythmical system, see Selg, P. *Vom Logos menschlicher Physis*, p. 505 ff., and Selg, P. (ed.) *Rudolf Steiner – Quellentexte fuer die Wissenschaften*. Band 3. *Physiologische Menschenkunde*, p. 386 ff.

14 See Selg, P. *Vom Logos menschlicher Physis*, p. 613 ff., and Selg, P. (ed.) *Rudolf Steiner – Quellentexte fuer die Wissenschaften*. Band 3. *Physiologische Menschenkunde*, p. 185 ff.

15 See the methodologically exemplary monograph by Hans Mueller-Wiedemann *Mitte der Kindheit. Das neunte bis zwoelfte Lebensjahr. Beitraege zu einer anthroposophischen Entwicklungspsychologie.* Stuttgart 1973.

16 "From second dentition to sexual maturity, the child is fully occupied in aesthetically taking in the surroundings; an aesthetic way, full of love, of taking in the surroundings." (218, 232, also v.i.).

17　Concerning Rudolf Steiner's concept of the system of metabolism and limbs, see Selg, P. *Vom Logos menschlicher Physis*, p. 475 ff., and Selg, P. (ed.) *Rudolf Steiner – Quellentexte fuer die Wissenschaften. Band 3. Physiologische Menschenkunde*, p. 327 ff.

18　"[...] Then, after puberty, falling ill radiates [...] out from inside, from the systems of movement and digestion. [...] Now we can also see from pathology that in adults sickness radiates out, above all, from the metabolic system—even a migraine is a metabolic disease; this diseases then does not radiate from the head, whereas in children everything comes from the head." (306, 157/69). See also Selg, P. (ed.) *Rudolf Steiner – Quellentexte fuer die Wissenschaften. Band 3. Physiologische Menschenkunde*, p. 231 ff.

19　"[...] Our head, actually organized for the sphere beyond earth, would not be able to take in directly the strong forces that try to shoot into it from our metabolism, as a vehicle for the will. These forces must first gather themselves up. They must first come to a halt until they are adequately filtered, adequately diluted, and made into soul, to make themselves felt in the head. They go through this stage at the end of the second seven-year period, when will-powers pile up in the laryngeal organization; when they shoot up in the human being to such effect that they actually make themselves felt in the changing voice in the male organization—this shows itself in a somewhat different way in the female organization. These are the powers of will, which come to a halt before they shoot up into the head. We can therefore say: at the end of the second seven-year period, the powers of will accumulate in our speech organization. They are then sufficiently filtered, sufficiently made into soul, so as to make themselves felt in the head organization. Once we have reached sexual maturity, and also encounter the transformation of speech which runs parallel to this, we have reached the point where idea and will can work together through the head in the earthly human being" (201, 150).

20　Concerning developmental physiology in the change in

speech at maturation, see Rudolf Steiner's differentiated statements in the chapter "Die Kraeftedynamik des puberalen Stimmwechsels und die innerliche Aneignung gesprochener Sprache" in Selg, P. *Vom Logos menschlicher Physis*, p. 620 ff. It should also be noted that Steiner described the processes of sexual maturation in the whole organism as a general metamorphosis in childhood speech development ("The phenomena of sexual maturity, taking hold of the whole human being, developing a relationship, as it were, between the whole person and the environment, are anticipated, I'd say in another metamorphosis at the moment when the child's speech develops" 76, 134, lecture of April 7, 1921) and then, in Dornach on March 11, 1923, he made known, for the first time, the spiritual implications of the juvenile speech organizations. Looking back on the development and significance of speech in the first and second seven-year periods, referring to the night-time aftereffects of speech heard and spoken, he said then: "Until the seventh year of life, the echoes that live in the sleeping child's soul from going to sleep to waking up again are extraordinarily dependent on the human environment. Anything the father, mother, and other people around the child live out as their life of feeling, willing, and thinking in the words that the child hears echoes on in the child's soul when the child is sleeping. This young soul is wholly given up to anything put into words out of the heart and soul of those people. There, the feelings that the child experiences through the speech of the adults, the will impulses, and thoughts connect closely with the sounds. The child simply is wholly given up to everything that is experienced. This is less so in the second period of life, from the seventh to the fourteenth year, though it is still the case to a high degree. But with sexual maturity, with the fourteenth year, something very special begins. The element from speech that lives in the sleeping soul, by its own nature, becomes such that it wants to enter into a relationship with the spiritual world. It is thus something most peculiar. One could say that until the seventh year of life the child wants to communicate even in sleep with anything heard from the people around; this is so in a sense also from the seventh to the fourteenth year, only then it enters more into the actual soul life of the surroundings, The child enters more into the external aspects of life up until the seventh year. After the fourteenth year, however, once sexual life begins, a need arises for the sleeping human soul to communicate with spirits in the other world in the echo of speech, which lives on in sleep. As I said this is very peculiar. People are not aware of this in ordinary life, but in sleep the need arises for the inner life to let the speech element of earthly life echo on in such a way that the world of archangels, Archangeloi, can take pleasure in it. We can indeed say that the need arises for human beings to communicate when asleep with the archangelic world through the element of speech, which remains as an echo of external earth speech. The day's words then echo on in a strange way: all that is vowel is inwardly deepened, all that is consonant, arising from forms, is set into motion to the level of becoming tangible objects. This is the living experience. And the sleeping souls would feel unhappy if those echoes were not a speech that would now sound similar to what sounds from the other side, the speech of the archangels. Harmony is possible between the echoes of speech sounding into sleep and the speech of the archangelic world sounding out of the astral from all sides in the universe. Human beings develop in such a way in the "I" and the astral body that from the fourteenth year of life they must be in converse with angels and archangels between going to sleep and waking up, needing to communicate with angels and archangels. This is a profound secret in human life. (222, 13 ff: concerning the significance of speech sustained by ideals [see continuing text and Note 37] or embodying them with regard to the higher hierarchies, see Rudolf Steiner's further statements in the same lecture of March 11, 1923, but also those of March 12, 1923 [GA 222}, April 18, 1923 [GA 224], May 18, 1923 {GA 225], and May 23, 1923 [GA 224] which take the subject further).

21 Concerning the evolution and further development of the larynx and heart in the future, see Rudolf Steiner's statements on this in Selg, P. *Vom Logos menschlicher Physis*, p. 171 ff.

22 See Rudolf Steiner's comprehensive lecture on the heart, May 26, 1922 (GA 212), and the way the subject was presented in later lectures by Steiner in Selg, P. *"Mysterium cordis." Von der Mysterienstaette des Menschenherzens. Studien zu einer sakramentalen Physiologie des Herzorgans. Aristoteles – Thomas von Aquin – Rudolf Steiner*. Dornach 2003. In the whole physiological context, one must also take note that according to Rudolf Steiner, the second hierarchy—Exusiai, Dynamis, Kyriotetes—begins to be active as young people enter into the time of earthly maturation, and thus into the sphere of action of that hierarchy central to development on earth ("With the fourteenth year of life, the second hierarchy begins to be active—Exusiai, Dynamis, Kyriotetes" 236, 192), not only inscribing their own actions and intentions into an individual's destiny or evolving karma, but also activating the individual past-karma and its activity ("[...] which is why one's own karma only begins to take effect after sexual maturity." 316, 153). Discussing the contemporary youth movement, Rudolf Steiner said in Breslau on June 12, 1924: "What, ultimately, is the intention of this youth movement? Well, it wants to take hold of this cloud-like human being who emerges into sexual maturity, who lives in the human being. Young people want to be educated so that they can grasp this human being. But who is this human being? What does this human being really represent? What, as it were, emerges from this human body which we have seen develop in the physiognomy, in the gestures, and with whom we can also feel how pre-earthly existence assumes form in the second period of life, from second dentition to sexual maturity? What is now emerging as something entirely foreign; what is shooting forth from human beings when, after gaining sexual maturity, they become aware of their freedom and go toward other people,

seeking to join forces from an inner impulse that has established this trait in them, inexplicable to themselves and others, this quite specific trait of the inner human being? What is this human being, this second human being that now appears? It is the one who lived in the previous life on Earth and now enters into the present life on Earth as a shadow. Humanity will gradually learn to take account of karma in this strange element entering into human life at around the time of sexual maturity. At the moment in life when individuals become able to produce a human entity of their own kind, the impulses also arise in them which they represented in earlier lives on Earth" (239, 211 ff.). Two months before he spoke in Breslau, Rudolf Steiner also said emphatically in a lecture he gave in Bern that young people also experience this different quality of life's events—affecting them and partly created by them—as follows: "Before [this event], the individual is more or less *in it all* quite generally, feeling life on earth to be like someone familiar. Now, however, with sexual maturity, individual events come in such a way that the young person senses their destiny-quality. Taken in terms of destiny, life only then becomes the person's true individual life." (309, 67; concerning the incipient influence of "old" destiny at the level of the ether body in the second seven-year period, see also Rudolf Steiner's lecture of November 13, 1916 [GA 172].).

23 This process, preceding or moving toward maturity for earth, in which the astral body enters into the physical and etheric organism, was described as follows on August 18, 1924 in Torquay: "The [astral body] really only develops full activity upon sexual maturity. It is only then that it is really wholly active within the human organism. [...] Between birth and the second dentition, the etheric body is, as it were, drawn out of the physical body; between the seventh and fourteenth years, it then gradually attracts the astral body; and when it has been completely drawn in—no longer just loosely connected but wholly and closely inside physical and etheric body—then the human being has

reached the point of sexual maturity in life. – In boys, the change of voice shows that the astral body is now completely in the larynx; in girls, the development of other organs, breasts, and so on, shows that the astral body has now entered fully. The astral body slowly enters into the living human body from all sides. – The lines and directions it follows are the nerves. The astral body follows the nerve-fibres from the outside to the inside. There it gradually begins—first from the periphery, from the skin, and then inwardly—to draw itself together, filling the whole body. Before this, it is a loose cloud in which the child lives. Then it contracts, closely taking hold of all the organs, connecting chemically with the organism, to put it crudely, with the physical and etheric tissue" (311, 99). The physical and etheric vital function is progressively taken hold of by the astral body, and Steiner referred to this repeatedly and in different aspects (see Selg, P. *Vom Logos menschlicher Physis*, p. 622 ff.). The relationship between astrally determined respiratory and neural processes is established in the course of the second seven-year period ("The whole of this breathing as it follows the nerve fibres will only be wholly engaged in the physical body, where the astral body is concerned, in the course of time—when the child is just of school age, between the second dentition and sexual maturity." 311, 100 f.), and culminates in sexual maturity. Of this, Rudolf Steiner said on August 7, 1921, in Dornach, that it is literally "inhaled" with astral powers: "We actually inhale the principle which gives us sexual maturity, and also in the widest sense makes it possible for us to enter into a relationship of loving embrace with the world. This we actually inhale. Every natural process has a spiritual aspect: an element of spirit and soul. This element of spirit and soul enters into us with the breathing process. It can only enter when these powers gain the soul qualities that were actively involved in the organism before, and which cease to be active upon the second dentition. Then the principle that wants to come from the breathing process flows into the human being." (206, 100)

24 In this sense, Steiner also emphasized in his first medical course in Dornach that in adolescence, "the astral body itself" must "enter into the right relationship to the physical body and etheric body" (312, 140). In a lecture given to theologians eighteen months later in Dornach, he said of the configuration of the bodies which is balancing out: "The second process of evolution [after the process of birth] in our life is the one which shows itself in its full power when the individual gains sexual maturity, when the physical body and the ether body have reached a certain degree of development, and the astral body begins especially to enter into development; that is, when principles that always separate in the sleep state enter into a new relationship. In the sleep state, the physical and etheric bodies stay in the bed, and the astral body and the "I" leave of them. Human life therefore consists in a close relationship between the physical and etheric bodies, and a looser connection initially between these two and astral body and "I." In the waking state, these four are interpenetrating; but in the sleep state, astral body and "I" are out of the physical and etheric bodies, with the connection being relatively loose. This situation undergoes a certain modification, however, upon reaching maturity [in the fourteenth, fifteenth and sixteenth years]. Only then does interaction develop with the principle that in sleep is separated from the living physical body, which stays in bed. The right harmony only comes during the fourteenth, fifteenth and sixteenth years. There, the individual is taken hold of by an inner strength, and then penetrates the living physical body with the spiritual and soul principles; that is, the astral and "I"-nature. Outwardly this shows itself in the achievement of sexual maturity, which is merely the most outward revelation of a complete transformation of the whole human being. This process, which here begins as an evolution, may be referred to as maturation" (343, 258). With reference to pathophysiology, Rudolf Steiner said in a lecture on February 6, 1919, that inner developmental deficits and problems in the concerted action of the astral and

etheric bodies are the real basis of crises in soul and psychiatric developments in adolescence (and hence at the age when schizophrenic and psychotic conditions reach a first peak of manifestation). In the lecture he said, e.g.: "In the seventeenth, or eighteenth years—years of crisis—it is [then] apparent that the bodies did not develop properly: that the astral body did not harmonize with its drives and desires, nor the etheric body with the corresponding skills and habits. Outer and inner developments are then out of tune with each other. In less severe cases, it then happens that people lose their inner equilibrium, and it is also possible for the inner life to break down completely" (118, 190).

25 As Rudolf Steiner stressed even in June 1906, the partial separation of the astral organization from the processes that develop and configure the living body comes earlier in girls than in boys ("The astral body only comes free from the fourteenth to the twenty-first year. At sexual maturity it begins to go out, a bit earlier in girls than in boys." 94, 132).

26 Concerning the general issue of a tendency where "I"-powers are excessively absorbed by the rest of the human organization in puberty and adolescence ("We must try, through education, to avoid anything that makes the "I" absorbed too much by the organization, thus becoming too dependent on it" 302a, 56), see among other things Rudolf Steiner's central discussion in the lectures of September 22, 1920 (GA 302a), and also the earlier references on January 12, 1911 (GA 60).

27 Concerning the need to conceptually penetrate learning content that has been taken in through the form of images and made one's own earlier on (in the second seven-year period), Rudolf Steiner wrote: "Up to sexual maturity, the young person should acquire the treasures that humanity has thought about, doing so by memorizing them; after this comes the time when the young person must penetrate conceptually the things that were well-imprinted in the memory. Human beings should therefore not merely remember what they have grasped, but also grasp the things they know; that

is, what they have made their own through memory, as a child does with language and speech" (34, 336).

28 "You can do nothing worse to someone than to awaken their powers of judgment too early. We can only form an opinion once we have stored up substance within us for judgment, for comparison. If people form their own opinions before this, they will lack a proper basis. All bias in life, all empty 'confessions of faith' based on a few crumbs of knowledge, and on that basis aiming to judge living ideas often experienced by humanity over long periods of time, are due to errors made in this direction in education" (34, 342).

29 On November 19, 1922, Steiner pointed out in London that adolescents are only physiologically able to participate in the peripheral processes of the sensory organization from inside, and with their own powers of will, upon reaching sexual maturity (see also Note 9), adding in generally anthropological terms: "Taking part in the sensory organization from inside makes people intellectual. We only become such intellectual people once sexual maturity has been reached. *It is only then that we have the right facilities to judge the world according to the intellect. For to judge intellectually is to judge personally, out of inner freedom. This we only come to once we have entered into the period of sexual maturation*" (218, 233; italics are the author's).

30 Rudolf Steiner spoke about the difference between "judgment based on moral feeling" and "moral and intellectual judgment" on November 19, 1922 (GA 218). On July 3, 1917, for example, he emphasized that the child's "judgment based on moral feeling" in the second seven-year period shows the unconscious or semi-conscious level of an "instinctive" tendency (towards or away from)—indeed of an educationally guided or encouraged "instinct"—and must subsequently be conceptually penetrated or "rationalized" in puberty and adolescence (GA 176).

31 "Whereas one has taken children, in self-understood authority, to the moral principle, so that this lives in their world of feelings, duty works its way out of the individual's own

inner life once sexual maturity is reached. That is the health aspect" (310, 118).

32 "Human freedom means that human beings find the impulses that guide and drive them in life within themselves" (83, 18).

33 In generally educational terms, Rudolf Steiner said in Stuttgart on April 10, 1924: "[...] I will only truly educate [a human being] if I do not intervene in his or her self, but wait until this self is able to intervene itself in what I have provided as a basis in education. And so I live with the child for the moment when I can say: There the self is born in its freedom; I have merely prepared the ground so that it may become aware of itself." (308, 74) In even clearer and more radical terms, it was put to the teachers at the Stuttgart Waldorf School on June 22, 1922: "We can be extraordinarily helpful to ourselves there if, I would say, [...] we meditate on and profoundly develop the awareness that all education fundamentally has nothing at all to do with the true individual nature of a person, that as educators and teachers it is essentially our task to approach the individual with reverence, offering the opportunity for individual nature to follow its own laws of development, whilst we merely clear away the obstacles to development that lie in the physical and bodily aspect and in living body and soul; that is, in the physical and etheric bodies. All we are called upon to do is to clear away the hindrances in physical and bodily aspects, and in living body and soul, and let the individual nature develop freely. Any insights we convey to the children should essentially only serve to take the living body—both the physical body and the etheric body—so far, that the individual is then able to develop in freedom" (302a, 8). Concerning the encouragement of the above-mentioned individual powers of moral intuition, it was finally said in Stuttgart on March 26, 1923: "[...] If one has [...] implanted the right moral sympathies and antipathies in the child while the most important will developments are taking place "underground"—without impinging on the moral will by

giving commandments—the individual, free will can manifest such that, after reaching puberty, the person can be acknowledged as an independent fellow human being. The individual is then able to transform, to metamorphose, the gift of moral sympathies and antipathies, granting them a new orientation in moral impulses that now come from the individual's own being" (304a, 49 ff.).

34 "One soul freely giving itself to the other—this must develop from something; it must first find its way out of an initial dedication based on a feeling for authority. This is the pupil stage for all social love in life, during which we first go through the feeling for authority. People are empty of love, antisocial, when the feeling for authority does not live in teaching and education between the seventh and the fourteenth or fifteenth years" (192, 193 ff.).

35 As Rudolf Steiner put it in another lecture on education, the experience of beauty and its encouragement through art in the second seven-year period also makes it possible to relate more freely to the bodily changes connected with sexual maturation: "In finding the world beautiful, human beings will again and again be able to relate to their own living body in a free way, not to be harassed by it, which is really what eroticism consists of" (302, 78).

36 See Note 22.

37 In Berlin on February 28, 1911, Rudolf Steiner said about the essential nature of the idealist: "Mentally and spiritually, the characteristic of an idealist is that his ideas are greater, more comprehensive, than his actions. Take note, an idealist is someone whose intentions, ideas, are greater than what can possibly be done on the physical plane" (124, 131 ff.). A year later, in the same place, he said again, more explicitly: "It is the very nature of the ideal that we strive after it and always have the feeling, especially when young, that our whole behavior and our whole nature is far from adequate compared to the ideal; that the ideal is like a heavenly image above us, and we strive after it knowing that we will in fact never reach it." (61, 418) As Steiner put it in an earlier lecture

relating to adolescence, in developmental psychology and physiology, prime importance is not attached to the actual realization of the ideals of one's youth, but to making the *powers* inherent in them available here and now. "These are positive, vital energies that wake us up if well cultivated, making the astral body certain and confident for the life ahead." (10 Mar. 1908; quoted from Huber-Reebstein E./ Huber H. *Ausfuehrungen Rudolf Steiners zum Verstaendnis des 3. Jahrsiebtes in seinem allgemeinen Vortragswerk.* Band 2. Stuttgart 1982, p. 343.) See also Note 20.

38 Using this concept, Steiner said on 5 January 1922 in Dornach in front of teachers from many European countries: "Just think of how much our whole civilization is lacking in this respect. Ask yourselves if there are not many people nowadays who use the telephone, the tram, you could even say the steamboat, without having an idea of what is actually happening in a steam boat, in a telephone, or when a tram is moving. The human being of our time is surrounded by things that he does not understand. This might seem unimportant to those who believe that only what happens in the conscious life is relevant. Certainly, one can live well in the conscious life if one just buys a tram ticket and goes to the station to which one wants to go; or if one receives a wired message without having the slightest idea how this message has been conveyed, without ever having seen a Morse telegraph. For our ordinary consciousness, so much as we can say, this makes no difference; but for that which happens in the depths of the human soul, it does make a difference: *the human being in a world, that he makes use of but that he does not understand, is like a human being in a prison without a window through which he could look out into open nature.*" (303, 254 ff.; author's emphasis). Already in one of the first lectures given by Rudolf Steiner for the teachers at the opening of the Stuttgart Waldorf School, he pointed out: "The worst thing is to live in a world created by human beings, without showing any interest in this world." (294, 162; cf. also further down in the text, and note 40.)

39 Notice by Rudolf Steiner, quoted from Karl-Martin Dietz: *Erziehung in Freiheit*. [Education in Freedom] p. 72.

40 Rudolf Steiner referred to this social aspect of the initiation into the living surrounding of the young person that was mentioned above in his lecture of 15 August 1923 in Ilkley, where he said: "Just think of how many people nowadays enter a tram carriage without knowing how it is made to move, what mechanism it uses. There are even people who see trains passing by every day, and have no idea how the train engine works. This means, however, that these people live in the world surrounded by many things that have been developed by human ingenuity, which the human mind has invented, but they do not take part in this ingenuity. It is the beginning of an antisocial life if we ignore those things in our surroundings which human ingenuity has created, if we don't have at least a general understanding of them. [...] In the Waldorf School, we start connecting the young person from the fourteenth or fifteenth year onward, with the things that the human mind has brought about. By doing this, we place them firmly into the social life." (307, 196 ff.) Rudolf Steiner asks us, moreover, to consider that the education of the participating will toward "love for work and love for doing" (or "love for all that one does oneself") that is meant to develop through the relevant school events and projects, is of foremost social importance for the "loving devotion to what one does oneself," which can therefore be understood and practiced as an "understanding of what the other does." (306, 130/132).

41 Cf. Note 22.

42 As early as 1898 Rudolf Steiner wrote: "The young people should not believe in our 'truths,' but in our personality." (31, 233 f.)

43 It should be noted here that the child's real individuality, his individual soul-being, is, of course, already active and perceptible during the first two seven-year periods right down into his physiology (with regard to the gradual "anchoring" of the "I" in the physical, etheric, and astral during the first

three seven-year periods (see Rudolf Steiner's lecture of 22nd September 1920 [GA 302a]); still, one must not forget that, with the beginning of adolescence, a further individuality and destiny principle (see note 22) manifests itself increasingly in world-related deeds and interpersonal relationships. With regard to the influence of the individuality forces on the activities that form and change the body during the second seven-year period and during the transition to adolescence, Rudolf Steiner said on June 25, 1924 in Dornach: "Especially in the child, we must [...] distinguish between the inherited body and that which appears as a consequence of the inherited body in the individual body. The individual body, which is the one we can consider to be the real personality body of the human being, develops gradually. And between the ages of seven and fourteen, the individuality does most of the work it is capable of doing; either it keeps the upper hand over the forces of inheritance, and the human being develops while experiencing the change of teeth, thus showing that he works his way away from the forces of inheritance, *or* the individuality completely succumbs to the forces of inheritance, to that which is included in the model. This means that the inherited similarity with the parents continues beyond the seventh year. This depends on the individuality, not on the forces of inheritance. [...] Now, the young person between seven and fourteen years of age experiences a growing and developing which brings to strong expression the individuality that the human being has brought with him. This means that the young person is relatively isolated from the outer world during this time. This time particularly offers the opportunity to observe the wonderful development of the individuality. If the person were to continue this development later on, he would become terribly repelling; he would become dull in relation to the outer world. But during this time, he already develops his third body, which will appear along with sexual maturity. This body again will be formed under the influence of the forces that live in the earthly surroundings. [...] Now the human being achieves earthly-maturity and takes into himself that which is foreign. He acquires the ability to not become dull in relation to his surrounding. Before this, the opposite sex makes no impression on him, nor do the rest of his surroundings." (317, 17 ff.) From adolescence onward, the young person exposes his inner being to the world, and creates with the processes that change his body the conditions for his real "I" to gradually take effect, so that by the time he has reached his 21st year, it has grown up to "complete inner intensity." (107, 296) Only then, said Rudolf Steiner, can the individual stand in the world "as an independent, free being" (58, 163).

44 In an inconspicuous aside, Rudolf Steiner once said during a lecture on educating adolescents: "If one goes on a school trip with these children, one has conversations with individuals according to their individual orientation. One says to them: how do you think you will do this? How do you think you will do that? One refers to the future and includes the idea of purpose and aim into life." (302, 83) Rudolf Steiner spoke about a necessary education, or a pedagogically supported and encouraged "self-education to idealism," on 11 February 1919 in Zurich (193, 62).

45 Generally speaking, Rudolf Steiner saw the meticulous study of individual students as the main object of faculty meetings (as the "soul" of all teaching)—"so that this concentration on the child's individuality would form the essence of what the teachers would learn themselves in the course of these meetings" (311, 68). Still today, it is most helpful and instructive to study Rudolf Steiner's conferences with the teachers in view of the included child studies, even though the stenographic notes are not always complete and additional information about the children and adolescents that are discussed would be essential. But despite these limitations, they allow important insights into Rudolf Steiner's principles of how to develop an understanding for individual students. They also show in general how central a place within the school life Steiner allocated to the deepening anthroposophic study for the development of right under-

standing and support for individual students. ("And that is what the faculty meetings are there for. They are there to study the human being and to thus allow a constant flow of knowledge of the human being to penetrate the life of the school. In the faculty meetings, we study the school. The most important thought is that the faculty meetings are an ongoing, continuous teacher training." 311, 128)

46 Cf. the collection of biographical notes and characteristics of the individual teachers: *Der Lehrerkreis um Rudolf Steiner in der ersten Waldorfschule 1919-1925*. [The circle of teachers around Rudolf Steiner in the first Waldorf School] by Johannes Tautz and Gisbert Husemann (Stuttgart 1977).

47 On August 25, 1922, during a public pedagogical conference in Oxford, Rudolf Steiner described the situation that had led to the entire 10th grade of the Stuttgart Waldorf School approaching him in the spring of 1922 (see above): "One day when I was at the Waldorf School in order to give directions on teaching and education, something I can unfortunately only do sporadically, a girl of the upper grade came to me between lessons. She was in what I would call a state of repressed aggression and very upset, but still spoke with enormous inner conviction. She said: could we still today—it is very important—could the whole class (that is, the highest grade) still speak to you today. We only want to, however, if you want to, too. So, this kind of leader had taken her place at the front of the class and wanted to speak to me with the whole class being present. What was the reason? The reason was that the boys and girls had come to feel for themselves that they could not cope with the teachers any more. They found it difficult to deal with the teachers, to find the right way of going about it. – This was not because they were planning to plot against the teachers, but because, in the short time that the Waldorf School had existed, they had developed a deep love for their teachers. But these students of the upper grade, these fifteen- and sixteen-year-old boys and girls, they were terribly worried that they might lose this love or that it might diminish, because

of the new state of affairs that had developed. They were extremely worried." (305, 164 ff.)

48 "You know that with our Waldorf School method we achieve a lot with the children on the one hand, in an intellectual-spiritual way. And our students are indeed more advanced than pupils from other schools of the same age. That cannot be denied. From the 8th or 9th grade onward, the students in their entirety are actually a young section of humanity that is different from those students of other schools. The human being is, however, a holistic organism, which means that if one develops the spiritual-intellectual side of the young person, one also has to develop their moral-psychological side." (300c, 182 ff.)

49 In his pedagogical lectures, Rudolf Steiner many times pointed out that from puberty onward the previous "school-like treatment" (303, 220) was no longer appropriate for young people, meaning that one should no longer instruct them but consistently encourage them to actively use their own judgment.

50 Cf. Peter Selg: *Rudolf Steiner und Eugen Kolisko – Die Gründung der Waldorfschule und der erste Schularzt* [Rudolf Steiner and Eugen Kolisko – The founding of the first Waldorf School and the first school doctor], Dornach 2002, P. 17 ff.

51 Cf. Hans-Jürgen Hanke: *Karl Schubert. Lebensbilder und Aufzeichnungen* [Karl Schubert. Life pictures and notes]. Dornach 2004

52 Cf. note 45.

53 Coming from Zurich, Rudolf Grosse (1905-1994) joined class 10 of the Waldorf School. He later worked as a Waldorf teacher and curative teacher, and was, intermittently, leader of the teacher training seminar at the Goetheanum, the Youth Section, and the Pedagogical Section. In 1966, he became chairman of the General Anthroposophical Society. In his brilliant reminiscences, *Erlebte Pädagogik. Schicksal und Geistesweg* (Dornach 1998), Rudolf Grosse described, among other things, Rudolf Steiner's meetings with class 12

at the time of their graduation. Rudolf Grosse's former fellow pupil, Karin Ruths-Hoffman (1904-1986), also gave an account of the meetings on April 10 and September 3, 1924. She went to school in Szopienice, Upper Silesia, and started a teacher training in Wrocaw, which she left to join class 12 of the Stuttgart Waldorf School, where she stayed from Easter 1923 until 1924. She became a Steiner teacher as well, and also worked for aid organizations in prisons and at the Rudolf Steiner Seminar in Järna, Sweden. Compared to Rudolf Grosse's account, hers is less detailed and, in places, not as precise. The corresponding passage can be found in the essay "Aus der Waldorfschülerschaft" [From the Waldorf students] which she wrote for the anthology *Wir erlebten Rudolf Steiner. Erinnerungen seiner Schüler,* Stuttgart 1956 [We experienced Rudolf Steiner. Memories of his students], edited by Dora Krück von Poturzyn. She wrote: "The time of the graduation came closer. The Waldorf School was not even five years old, so nobody in my class had gone all the way through, and we all felt that we would rather start again than leave already. Then, one dusky afternoon when we left our classroom, reluctantly as always, one of us had an idea. I think it was Bossi, the Italian boy. 'Could we not ask for a meeting with Rudolf Steiner before we have to leave?' We were promised it. – The sun shone into the teachers' room, all our teachers were sitting along the walls, around us, while we were asked to take our seats at the conference table, at the head of which Rudolf Steiner, accompanied by Ita Wegman, sat. A leader of humankind, the most comprehensive mind of our times—no, of entire eras—he took us, a bunch of high school graduates, seriously enough to listen to every single one of us as an individual. But first, he addressed us all together. He said that whenever we had to make important decisions in our lives, the spirit of our school would stand behind us and whisper the right advice into our ears. 'The conversations with your fellow pupils will one day be the most important thing for you, something you can always fall back on.' Then we were asked to say what we wanted to be.

He said he could imagine that a number of us wanted to become Waldorf teachers, not all at this school, of course, for our dear teachers surely were not going to die so soon. (He pointed to the walls where we saw our beloved teachers, like noble fruit along a trellis). And indeed, our best pupil, the smartest mathematician in any case, declared that he wanted to be a teacher. But he was advised to train for commerce. 'Go to England and America—have a look how they go about it—and then come back and do it as it should be done *here*.' Another one wanted to become an architect. For him, Rudolf Steiner suggested technology. He should try to bring the artistic element that he was striving for into the technical world. To two of us who were interested in teaching, he advised to study physics, chemistry and philosophy. To one girl who wanted to become a kindergarten teacher, he said that the single most important factor was that the children love her. A kindergarten teacher could be quite dull.... With hindsight, it seems to me that Rudolf Steiner, while he lovingly responded to our adolescent life-problems, also tried to put us straight so that, above all, no spiritual arrogance would arise. The following example might illustrate this even better. The oldest girl in the class, who was already engaged to be married, had originally wanted to study medicine, but we were all so enthused by the radically new Waldorf approach to education, that going on to a conventional university seemed to us like a step backwards. 'I could not go on from the Waldorf School to study medicine. I would die!' our friend exclaimed emphatically. 'But why?' answered Rudolf Steiner, pointing amicably to Dr. Wegman next to him who was a physician. 'She is still in a good condition...' He continued: 'In your situation (as a soon-to-be-married woman) it would be good to study eurythmy therapy, because that is not a full-time profession' (It was not at the time). Then he turned to those of us who were racking our brains over 'our highly spiritual future tasks.' 'In any case, my dear young ladies, it would be the most terrible thing that could happen to the Waldorf School if it produced nothing but old maids. I hope you all want to marry as well.' Almost outraged, I exclaimed: 'But, dear Dr. Steiner, getting married is not a profession!' 'Why not? It is even officially recognized.' 'But men also get married and have a profession.' 'Well, I was only alluding to one particular case.' – To a girl who wanted to become a nurse he said: 'That is a selfless profession. The patients in the Arlesheim hospital will not suddenly be cured because there is an interesting lecture up at the Goetheanum that the nurse would like to go and listen to.... A good nurse has to have something about her, through which the patients feel better as soon as she enters the room.' To a girl who wanted to be an artist, he suggested that she should go to Dornach. At this point, we also talked about the fact that the Goetheanum could not yet replace a university education in the way that the Waldorf School had come to replace a 'conventional' school. During this conversation it became clear to me, however, that Rudolf Steiner saw it as desirable to inaugurate a real school for higher education. When he suggested that we should come back to Stuttgart in the autumn to share our first life experiences, the present meeting seemed to me like the beginning of something new. I thought he also said that we should come back every year during our holidays in order to work with our former teachers, under their guidance, as a kind of complementary higher education course. – In September 1924, we had our second and last meeting with Rudolf Steiner. He listened attentively to our stories, and I remember that he seemed particularly pleased when one of our fellow students told us about his work in a factory, and described how the different departments had a character of their own, depending on whether they were processing timber or iron. He responded to this and began to talk to us about threefoldness. 'The idea of threefoldness is not dead,' he said, 'It just has not been understood yet. And I hope that an understanding for threefoldness will arise from the circle of Waldorf students.' That's what I seem to remember. – When one of our fellow students mentioned that he was planning to travel to South America in order to do scientific research in his subject, he was told that whatever one studied, whether it was plants or stones, one should not look for them in museums and artificial plantations but in their natural surroundings. – We were then invited to come to the pedagogical youth conference, which was to take place in November. But this conference did not happen as planned. Already on September 28, Rudolf Steiner gave his last lecture, and he was not to be part of the future autumn gatherings of former Waldorf students that he himself had instigated. – In the early April of 1925, some former Waldorf students met in the 'Schreinerei' in Dornach. Without having planned it, we found ourselves together at the entrance to the studio where the earthly sheath of our teacher was laid out. We were allowed to enter. The breath of life in death wafted through the stillness of the room, where the greatest man of our times lay beneath his work—the statue of the representative of humankind. – When we had left the Waldorf School, he had given us a verse to accompany us through life, which we had listened to, standing upright. Later on, we could ask him for this verse in writing, and at our last meeting he had urged us to meditate with it intensively—we would soon experience its effect. This verse enhanced and sealed the fact that our youth education stood under the leadership of the spirit, and that what our hearts were allowed to receive would be reflected on the width of our life paths, and retained in the depth of memory."

54   The words by Rudolf Steiner which Rudolf Grosse quoted during his speech of March 27, 1924, had obviously not been stenographed and were not part of the address given at the general monthly festival (cf. 298, 198 ff.), but in another speech two years earlier (at the beginning of the school year) Rudolf Steiner had put it like this: "It occupies the teacher's mind day and night, and he tries to find out how it will be in life once ten or twenty years will have passed. You will need clarity in order to approach your life in the right way."

55   Transcript of lecture notes with slight grammatical corrections (Ita Wegman Archives). Eugen Kolisko (1893-1939)

was a physician and scientist held in high esteem by Rudolf Steiner. From the spring of 1920, he taught at the Stuttgart Waldorf School, and from the fall of 1921 he was also school doctor. (see Selg, P. *Eugen Kolisko*, in *Anfänge anthroposophischer Heilkunst*. Dornach 2000, p. 123 ff., also Selg, P. (ed.): *Eugen Kolisko – Vom therapeutischen Charakter der Waldorfschule. Aufsätze und Vorträge*. Dornach 2002). Eugen Kolisko spoke regularly at the annual gatherings of former Waldorf students and their teachers, which Rudolf Steiner had encouraged ("come every year at this time to the school and share with your teachers what you have experienced in your lives. The teachers will then give you lectures on what they have researched in the meantime. In this way, a kind of school for further education in the spirit of the Waldorf School will be established" – see above) until he left the Stuttgart School in the summer of 1934.

56 Christoph Boy (1887-1934) was a teacher at the Stuttgart Waldorf School around 1921.

57 I first published this letter written by Ita Wegman (1876-1943), leader of the Medical Section at the Goetheanum and Rudolf Steiner's close assistant, to the Stuttgart Waldorf teacher Ernst Lehrs (1894-1979), in the weekly magazine *Das Goetheanum*, No. 31, August 1, 2004 (p. 7-9), with a comment that was slightly edited. My unabridged comment was: "At the beginning of 1931 Ita Wegman wrote a letter to Ernst Lehrs, five months after the great anthroposophical youth conference 'Kamp de Stakenberg' in which both of them had taken part as lecturers. More than 1000 liberal-minded young people had again come together for this camp from different countries in Europe, despite the already looming shadows of National Socialism. ("On foot, by bike, they arrived in many different ways, seven hundred young foreigners, three hundred members, a thousand all in all. It was staggering what sacrifices they had taken upon themselves to be able to be here. They had moved from town to town, taking on work on the way,

some had been on the road for weeks. Three hundred from Germany, two hundred from Holland, eighty from Britain, etc., one from China, one African girl, one Indian. I had never spoken so openly." W. J. Stein). The Dutch psychiatrist Willem Zeylmans van Emmichoven had opened the conference with the words: 'Many people are saying now: things have to change. They speak out of despair. One can sense that they want to throw everything over. One can understand this especially if one stands in front of them. But that is not the way to move forward. Because one could ask: what would a situation look like that was born out of such a subversive impulse? We believe that the future can only live if we understand what powers are necessary for our civilization. This leads to a spiritual understanding, and out of this understanding one will be able to say: "Now one can see that a metamorphosis is about to happen. It is not about new systems, it is about new human beings."' – Ita Wegman wrote to Ernst Lehrs at the beginning of 1931, a year that was to bring the dissolution of the Free Anthroposophical [Youth] Society. She wrote on January 20, five days after Maria Röschl's letter to Albert Steffen, in which the highly gifted leader of the Youth Section at the Goetheanum in Dornach resigned from her position, a fact of which Wegman was not yet aware when she wrote her letter. She wrote at a time when the youth initiatives that had started with such hope and determination, withdrew, or, rather, had to withdraw from an Anthroposophical Society that could not offer them real space or spiritual-historical understanding, but instead was getting hopelessly caught up in society-aggression, self-centeredness, and self-dissolution. Ita Wegman, who was at the time secretary of the esoteric council and who herself became a victim of these events, wrote at the beginning of a year in which Adolf Hitler would appoint Baldur von Schirach as youth leader of the NSDAP, ranking as a SA-group leader; a year in which the headquarters of the Hitler Youth was moved to Munich and the NS youth work became more centralized; a year in which the 'NS youth manifesto' was published, which began with the words: 'We, the young people of Germany, we, the generation of the future, we, as the youth of work and deed raise our right hand as a sign of the awakening Germany and pledge allegiance in the year of dishonor, infamy and the enslavement of our people: 1931. – We, who as children of the war have gained maturity and insight, lower the banners, commemorate our fathers and brothers who fell for a free Germany in the fields of honor. – We, who are of German blood and race, accuse! Against right and law Germany's youth who follow Adolf Hitler were wilfully persecuted and terrorized! We are ready to take on our rightful inheritance!' Shortly after this, Adolf Hitler was to seize power in Germany and put his own 'pedagogical' intentions into practice, which he had already energetically pursued since 1922 (by creating a strictly controlled youth organization). In 1933, he ordered all free youth organizations to be dissolved, and declared them illegal. From then on, there was to be only one Hitler Youth, whose endeavour it was to take over youth education and control it ideologically. This was largely put into practice. In Adolf Hitler's programmatic words: 'These young people must learn nothing else but to think and act as true Germans. We must get these boys into our organization at the age of 10 where they can, for the first time, breathe the fresh air. Four years later they move on to the Hitler Youth where we keep them for another four years. And then we will certainly not let them return into the clutches of the old creators of class thinking, but we put them straight into the party, the Labour Front, the SA or SS, the NSKK (National Socialist Motor Corps), and so on. If they are there for two or one and a half years and still have not become proper national socialists, we stick them into labour camps where they get drilled for a further six or seven months; all will be united under one symbol: the German spade. And if there is any hint of class conceit left in them, the Wehrmacht (Armed Forces) will take them on for another two or three years, after which we will send them right back to the SA, SS and so on, to prevent any kind of relapse. They will not be free again for the rest of their lives.' (December 12, 1938) – '*I have the feeling, that we do not fulfil our tasks as anthroposophists, if around us we see the needs of the human souls, and the needs of the children's souls in particular—which are snatched up by all sorts of organizations, who shape their young brains according to their maxims, so that later on there is no way of getting rid of what has been instilled in these children at this age—and fail to carry out what Rudolf Steiner wanted: to have schools where children are educated in the right way so that they can become truly human. And this does not really happen, because the Waldorf children are as exposed to the dangers of today's culture as are other children.*' Ita Wegman wrote these words to Ernst Lehrs just under eight years before Hitler's speech at Reichenberg, from which the above quote is taken. Two years later, just after the National Socialists had taken over Germany, she wrote in a letter to Erich Kirchner at the curative home Schloss Hamborn: '*That Hitler has come to power is bad, but nothing can be done about that now. We were too weak after all, and that will revenge itself bitterly.*' (February 5, 1933). – Ita Wegman's words to Ernst Lehrs are impressive and historically wide-awake, but over and above that, they constitute a valid, future-oriented document of an original Waldorf education; an education toward a 'free spiritual life.' They are, at the same time, an obligation, a perspective and a promise waiting to be honored. What Ita Wegman tried to re-awaken and inspire in 1931 also lived in Eugen Kolisko, who in 1930 was still active in the Stuttgart School, and considered it his duty as school doctor to meet with the students who would be graduating, to discuss with them the 'present world situation' and their place in it. This was in October 1930, i.e., between the 'Kamp de Stakenberg' and Ita Wegman's letter to Ernst Lehrs. – If we consider Rudolf Steiner's earlier indications in the courses on education and the faculty meetings of the Stuttgart School from 1919 to 1924, we see clearly that the *'fight for each soul'* and the acute awareness of the changing situation of the young people at that time were immanent prerequisites for a youth anthropology; i.e. they belong to the real—and therefore genuine-authentic—art of education that Rudolf Steiner had engraved, right from the beginning, as legacy into the Stuttgart Waldorf School. Again and again he pointed out how important it was, especially when teaching adolescents, to make a real connection with the students, and not to merely lecture. He repeatedly had personal conversations with the young people, and advised the teachers when they had questions. In October 1922, he had written to Edith Maryon at the Goetheanum: '[...] That I was absent from the school for so long has had negative effects. The teachers completely lost touch with the high school students. [...] If they were incapable! But that is not the case. The problem is that they are lacking enthusiasm; they are lacking active joy in their work. People want to keep doing the same things, they want routine; they want to be a heavy mass rather than an incentive. They are basically inert.' (263/1, 103) As all Waldorf teachers continued to do later on, Rudolf Steiner met—still in 1924, accompanied by Ita Wegman—the graduates, and highlighted with them their individual, professional, and biographical perspectives. Three years earlier, in the fall of 1921, he had encouraged teachers to offer students consultation times where philosophical questions, also of an anthroposophical nature, could be discussed openly, without undue anxiety. ('You cannot avoid that the consultations will touch on anthroposophy when you discuss philosophical questions. You can avoid it in religion, and that is difficult. In the consultations, you cannot avoid it. It is not necessary either.' 300b, 50). Rudolf Steiner always urged teachers to develop astute pedagogical awareness for the situation and the—conscious or unconscious—questions of young people, without cultivating, under any circumstances, an undifferentiated, pseudo-companionable atmosphere of equality. In the first years of the Waldorf School, Rudolf Steiner had urged teachers to be aware of any narrow-mindedness in Waldorf education; he wanted to educate teachers as well as students to be 'cosmopolitans' (300b, 211). He clearly foresaw all the possible corruptions of true Waldorf education ('It is easier to turn the good into its opposite than the bad' 300b, 159), and its failure, as a result, to fulfil its mission for humankind—the ingratiating pseudo-popularisation and spiritual trivialization as well as the potential sclerotization. Rudolf Steiner foresaw all this at the beginning of the 1920s, when he was faced with an already politically pressing present and future. He had, one can assume, a concrete picture of the students' future lives and sufferings, of the abysses and unavoidable dangers, the generational tasks, possibilities and errors. Ita Wegman's letter on youth education addressed to Ernst Lehrs, and written just six years after Rudolf Steiner's death, also has to be seen in this school-immanent context—its historical facticity, but also its ongoing validity, which Wegman wanted to keep awake or re-instigate, and which is still waiting to be truly realized. It can hardly be denied that Ita Wegman's remark that *'we have to be careful that we don't gradually lose the young people, those who used to attend the Waldorf School or those who are still going to the Waldorf School'* has, despite various youth initiatives in the anthroposophical world and individual developments within the Waldorf movement, lost nothing of its oppressive, mortifying, and certainly socially dangerous topicality. The situation of adolescents at the beginning of the twenty-first century is, as far as real inner dangers are concerned, more dramatic than ever, in an era where a highly technisized, thoroughly commercialised, and seductive materialism threatens to render any meaningful concepts and social intentions absurd, and to throw the *searching souls* described by Ita Wegman back into a substantial void. How we can really find and reach the subliminally and existentially working powers within the children and adolescents in the present time—away from metaphysical postulates and modernistic compromises—has remained an open and unanswered question in the Waldorf Schools. Together with Ita Wegman, we must assume that now is not the time to extend what is seen as Steiner education into practice by attempts at identity-searching and modernisation, but rather to implement an esoterically founded pedagogical method that is based on 'human development and human insight' (300b, 158 f.), and that will ultimately develop the organs through which the real spirit of time can actively empower and pedagogically guide the teachers in charge of the education. The education of adolescents—more specifically than children of other ages—has to do with the future, with future soul developments and world tendencies which are only there in seed-form today. This pedagogy becomes reality and competence to the same degree that the individual teacher develops within himself a perceptive and creative organ for the powers of the future; to the same degree that the teacher—esoterically speaking—begins to live and work in the light of Michael. Ita Wegman, at any rate, who was appointed by Rudolf Steiner as leader of the Medical Section and as associate ('second leader') of the School of Michael, was able to write this letter and point out possibilities and dangers 'in good time,' because she had undergone an advanced spiritual-esoteric schooling; she knew the Michaelic 'signs of the time' from the inside, and was therefore able to see and act. Without referring much to this dimension of her request and appealing foremost on pragmatic grounds to the extraordinarily gifted Ernst Lehrs—knowing that he, with Rudolf Steiner, had been instrumental in bringing about the 'Pädagogische Jugendkurs' [1922 lectures to young people, GA 217] and the Free Anthroposophical Society, but particularly also the esoteric youth circle—Ita Wegman lived in the firm knowledge that the great problems of civilization can only be solved or, at least, responsibly worked on if there is true inner schooling. She was fully familiar with Rudolf Steiner's far-reaching esoteric support for the faculty of teachers in Stuttgart, and also with those lines from the last letter he wrote to them just two weeks before his death, after he had sent them a last teachers' meditation written down in his studio: 'Therefore we want to strive more earnestly for unity in the spirit, as more is not possible. The Waldorf School might be a problem child, but more than anything it is also a landmark for the fruitfulness of anthroposophy in the spiritual life of humankind. If the teachers carry within their hearts the awareness of this fruitfulness, then the good spirits that are watching over this school can do their work, and the deeds of the teachers will be endowed with divine-spiritual power.' (260a, 405 f.) All these words and spiritual realities were standing behind Ita Wegman's often modest phrasing and expressions – '*We fight for each soul. We have to think of this, and the teachers have a great responsibility toward these souls.*' – What can also be seen as helpful, if not exemplary for the future, is Ita Wegman's general tone and attitude which should, at least, be marginally considered. She, who since Rudolf Steiner's death had again and again been accused in the extreme of attempting to seize and exert power, did not order or urge Ernst Lehrs when she addressed her existential, deeply felt concerns at him, but wrote in a style that left him free to make his own decision, a style that opened up a space for dialogue and responsible action, and that reflected, at the same time, true inner modesty and genuine morality: '*I hope you don't take it amiss that I wrote you this letter. All I meant to say is that I would like to hear from you what you think about this and what your experiences are.*'"

Literature Cited

a) Works by Rudolf Steiner in English, referred to in the text and notes

GA 34 — *The Education of Children.* Tr. not known. London: Theosophical Publishing Co. 1911. Also in GA 60 (v.i.).
GA 40 — *Truth-Wrought-Words.* Tr. Arvia MacKaye Ege. Spring Valley, NY: Anthroposophic Press 1979.
GA 55 — *Supersensible Knowledge.* Tr. Rita Stebbing. Hudson, NY: Anthroposophic Press 1987.
GA 58 — *Transforming the Soul.* vol 1. Tr. Pauline Wehrle. Formerly called *Metamorphosis of the Soul.* Forest Row, England: Rudolf Steiner Press 2005.
GA 60 — *The Education of the Child.* Tr. various. Hudson, NY: Anthroposophic Press 1996.
GA 76 — *The Fourth Dimension.* Tr. C. E. Creeger. Great Barrington, MA: Anthroposophic Press 2001.
GA 83 — *The Tension between East and West.* Tr. B. A. Rowley. London: Hodder&Stoughton 1963.
GA 94 — *An Esoteric Cosmology.* Tr. not known. Revised edition. Great Barrington, MA: SteinerBooks 2008.
GA 107 — *The Being of Man and His Future Evolution.* Tr. Pauline Wehrle. London: Rudolf Steiner Press.
GA 118 — *Reappearance of Christ in the Etheric.* Tr. Great Barrington, MA: Anthroposophic Press 2003.
GA 124 — *Background to the Gospel of St. Mark.* Tr. E. H. Goddard, D. S. Osmond. London/NY: Rudolf Steiner Press/Anthroposophic Press 1985.
GA 172 — *The Karma of Vocation.* Tr. O. D. Wannamaker, rev. G. Church. Hudson, NY: Anthroposophic Press 1984.
GA 176 — *Aspects of Human Evolution.* Tr. R. Stebbing. Hudson, NY: Anthroposophic Press 1987.

GA 193   *Esoteric Aspects of the Social Question.* Tr. Pauline Wehrle. London: Rudolf Steiner Press 2001.
GA 200   *New Spirituality & the Christ Experience of the Twentieth Century.* Tr. P. King. London/NY: Rudolf Steiner Press/Anthroposophic Press 1988.
GA 201   *The Mystery of the Universe.* Tr. G. & M. Adams, rev. M. Barton. London: Rudolf Steiner Press 2001.
GA 210   *Old and New Methods of Initiation.* Tr. J. Collis. London: Rudolf Steiner Press 1991.
GA 212   *The Human Heart.* Tr. not known. Spring Valley, NY: Mercury Press 1985.
GA 217   *Becoming the Archangel Michael's Companions.* Tr. R. M. Querido. Great Barrington, MA: SteinerBooks 2007. Formerly, *The Younger Generation.* Anthroposophic Press 1967.
GA 217a *Youth and the Etheric Heart.* Tr. Catherine Creeger. Great Barrington, MA: SteinerBooks 2007.
GA 218   *Waldorf Education and Anthroposophy* vol. 2. Tr. N. P. Whittaker & R. F. Lathe. Hudson, NY: Anthroposophic Press 1996.
GA 222   *The Driving Force of Spiritual Powers in World History.* Tr. D. S. Osmond, J. Collis. Toronto: Steiner Book Centre 1972.
GA 224   *Riddles of the Inner Human Being.* Tr. F. E. Dawson. NY/London: Anthroposophic Press/Rudolf Steiner Press 1941.
GA 236   *Karmic Relationships. Vol II.* Tr. George Adams. Revised by M. Cotterell, C. Davy and D. S. Osmond. London: Rudolf Steiner Press 1997.
GA 239   *Karmic Relationships. Vol. VII.* Tr. D. S. Osmond. London: Rudolf Steiner Press 1973.
GA 260a *Constitution of the School of Spiritual Science.* Tr. G. Adams, J. and S. Rudel. Rudolf Steiner Press 1980.
GA 293   *The Foundations of Human Experience.* Previously *Study of Man.* Tr. Robert F. Lathe and Nancy Parsons Whittaker. Hudson, NY: Anthroposophic Press 1996.
GA 294   *Practical Advice to Teachers.* Edited from a translation

by Johanna Collis. Great Barrington, MA: Anthroposophic press 2000.
GA 296 *Education as a Force for Social Change.* Tr. Robert F. Lathe and Nancy Parsons Whittaker. Hudson, NY: Anthroposophic Press 1997.
GA 298 *Rudolf Steiner in the Waldorf School.* Tr. Catherine Creeger. Hudson, NY: Anthroposophic Press 1996.
GA 300b *Faculty Meetings with Rudolf Steiner.* vol 1. Tr. Robert F. Lathe and Nancy Parsons Whittaker. Hudson, NY: Anthroposophic Press 1998.
GA 300c *Faculty Meetings with Rudolf Steiner.* vol 2. Tr. Robert F. Lathe and Nancy Parsons Whittaker. Hudson, NY: Anthroposophic Press 1998.
GA 302 *Education for Adolescents.* Tr. Carl Hoffmann. Hudson: Anthroposophic Press 1996. Also as *Supplementary Course – The Upper School.* Tr. not known. Sussex: College of Teachers, Michael Hall School. 1965.
GA 302a *Balance in Teaching.* Tr. Ruth Pusch and R. M. Querido. Great Barrington, MA: SteinerBooks 2007.
GA 303 *Soul Economy.* Tr. Roland Everett. Great Barrington, MA: Anthroposophic Press 2003.
GA 304a *Waldorf Education and Anthroposophy.* vol 1. Hudson, NY: Anthroposophic Press 1995.
GA 304b *Waldorf Education and Anthroposophy.* vol. 2. Tr. Nancy Whittaker, Robert Lathe, and Roland Everett. Hudson, NY: Anthroposophic Press 1996.
GA 305 *The Spiritual Ground of Education.* Revised edition. Great Barrington, MA: Anthroposophic Press 2004.
GA 306 *The Child's Changing Consciousness and Waldorf Education.* Tr. R. Everett. Hudson, NY: Anthroposophic Press 1988.
GA 307 *A Modern Art of Education.* Tr. Jesse Darrell, George Adams, Robert Lathe and Nancy Whittaker. Revised edition. Great Barrington, MA: Anthroposophic Press 2004.
GA 308 *Essentials of Education.* Tr. not known. Revised by Jesse Darrell. Further revised by the publisher. Hudson, NY: Anthroposophic Press 1997.

GA 309   *The Task of the Teacher.* Tr. H. Fox. Ilkeston: Educational Association n.d.
GA 310   *Human Values in Education.* Tr. V. Compton-Burnett. Great Barrington, MA: Anthroposophic Press 2005.
GA 311   *The Kingdom of Childhood.* Tr. H. Fox. Revised by the publisher. Hudson, NY: Anthroposophic Press 1995.
GA 312   *Introducing Anthroposophical Medicine.* Tr. C. E. Creeger. Hudson: Anthroposophic Press 1999. Also as *Spiritual Science and Medicine.* Tr. not known. London: Rudolf Steiner Press 1948.
GA 316   *Course for Young Doctors.* Rev. G. F. Karnow. Spring Valley: Mercury Press 1994.
GA 317   *Education for Special Needs.* Tr. M. Adams. Revised 1998. London: Rudolf Steiner Press.
GA 348   *From Comets to Cocaine.* Tr. A. R. Meuss. Forest Row, England: Rudolf Steiner Press 2001.

b) Secondary Literature

Ausubel, David P.: *Das Jugendalter.* München 1968.
Backe, Dieter: *Die 13- bis 18 jährigen.* Weinheim/Basel 1983.
Beichler, Christa/Klein, Elisabeth: *Vom Umgang mit Jugendlichen heute.* Schaffhausen 1977.
Blankenburg, Wolfgang: "Schizophrene Psychosen in der Adoleszenz." In: *Bull. Inst. Med.* Kumamoto University Nr. 48, 1983, S. 33ff.
Bühler, Charlotte: *Das Seelenleben des Jugendlichen.* Wien 1921
Dietler, Urs: *Jugend im Wandel. Pädagogik im Umbruch.* Heidelberg 2003.
Dietz, Karl-Martin: *Freiheit oder Anpassung—zur Aktualität des ethischen Individualismus.* Heidelberg 2001.
— *Erziehung in Freiheit. Rudolf Steiner über Selbständigkeit im Jugendalter.* Heidelberg 2003.
Doosry, Mona: *Zwischen Pubertät und Mündigkeit. Erziehungsaufgaben im Jugendalter.* Heidelberg 2003.
Eggers, Christian/Lempp, Reinhard/Nissen, Gerhard/Strunk, Peter: *Kinder- und Jugendpsychiatrie.* Berlin/Heidelberg/New York 1970.

Fucke, Erhard: Die *Bedeutung der Phantasie für Emanzipation und Autonomie des Menschen.* Stuttgart 1972.
— *Lernziel: Handeln können. Erfahrungen und Überlegungen zu einem erweiterten Bildungskonzept.* Frankfurt 1981.
— *Grundlinien einer Pädagogik des Jugendalters. Zur Lehrplankonzeption der Klassen 6 bis 10 an Waldorfschulen.* Stuttgart 1991.
Glueck, Sheldon und Eleanor: *Jugendliche Rechtsbrecher.* Stuttgart 1963.
Grosse, Rudolf: *Erlebte Pädagogik.* Dornach 1986.
Helsper, Werner, et al.: *Jugendliche Außenseiter. Zur Rekonstruktion gescheiterter Bildungs- und Ausbildungsverläufe.* Opladen 1991.
Huber-Reebstein, Elisabeth/Huber, Hellmut: *Ausführungen Rudolf Steiners zum Verständnis des 3. Jahrsiebtes in seinem allgemeinen Vortragswerk.* Stuttgart 1982.
Hurrelmann, Klaus/Rosewitz, Bernd/Wolf, Hartmut K.: *Lebensphase Jugend.* Weinheim/München 1985..
Iwan, Rüdiger: *Ansätze zur Entwicklung einer neuen Oberstufengestalt.* Stuttgart 2003.
— *Phantasie und Verantwortung. Projektunterricht als Anliegen der Waldorfpädagogik.* Heidelberg 2004.
Kiersch (Hg.): *Rudolf Steiner – Quellentexte für die Wissenschaften. Texte zur Pädagogik.* Dornach 2004.
Köhler, Henning: *Jugend im Zwiespalt.* Stuttgart 1990.
Eugen Kolisko: *Vom therapeutischen Charakter der Waldorfschule.* Dornach 2002.
Kretschmer, Wolfgang: *Reifung als Grund von Krise und Psychose.* Stuttgart 1972.
Leber, Stefan: *Die Menschenkunde der Waldorfpädagogik.* Stuttgart 1993.
Lempp, Reinhard: *Psychosen im Kindes- und Jugendalter. Eine Realitätsbezugsstörung.* Bern/Stuttgart/Wien 1973.
Muchow, Hans Heinrich: *Flegeljahre. Beiträge zur Psychologie und Pädagogik der "Vorpubertät".* Ravensburg 1950.
— *Sexualreife und Sozialstruktur der Jugend.* Hamburg 1959.
Müller-Wiedemann, Hans: *Mitte der Kindheit.* Stuttgart 1989.

Nissen, Gerd (Hg.): *Psychiatrie des Pubertätsalters.* Bern/Stuttgart/Wien 1985.
— *Psychische Störungen im Kindes- und Jugendalter.* Darmstadt 1986.
Rebmann, Hans: *Das dritte Jahrsiebt. Ausführungen Rudolf Steiners in seinen pädagogischen Vorträgen.* Stuttgart 1977.
Remschmidt, Helmut/Schmidt, Martin H.: *Kinder- und Jugendpsychiatrie in Klinik und Praxis.* Stuttgart/New York, 1985.
Schad, Wolfgang: *Erziehung ist Kunst. Pädagogik aus Anthroposophie.* Frankfurt 1986.
Schurian, Walter: *Psychologie des Jugendalters.* Opladen 1989.
Selg, Peter: *Vom Logos menschlicher Physis. Die Entfaltung einer anthroposophischen Humanphysiologie im Werk Rudolf Steiners.* Dornach 2000.
— *Rudolf Steiner – Quellentexte für die Wissenschaften. Band 3. Physiologische Menschenkunde.* Dornach 2004.
— *Krankheit, Heilung und Schicksal des Menschen. Über Rudolf Steiners geisteswissenschaftliches Pathologie- und Therapieverständnis.* Dornach 2004.
Sleigh, Julian: *Freiheit erproben. Das dreizehnte bis neunzehnte Lebensjahr.* Stuttgart 1992.
Spranger, Eduard: *Die Psychologie des Jugendalters.* Leipzig 1924.
Staley, Betty: *Pubertät.* Stuttgart 1995.
Steiner, Rudolf: *Gesamtausgabe* (GA). Dornach 1956ff.
Steinhausen, Hans-Christoph: *Psychische Störungen bei Kindern und Jugendlichen.* München/Wien 1987.
Suchantke, Andreas/Leber, Stefan/Schad, Wolfgang: *Die Geschlechtlichkeit des Menschen.* Stuttgart 1991.
Tautz. Johannes: *Lehrerbewusstsein im 20. Jahrhundert. Erlebtes und Erkanntes.* Dornach 1995.
Zimmermann, Heinz: *Was kann die Pädagogik des Jugendalters zur Willenserziehung beitragen.* Heidelberg 2002.

Ita Wegman Institute
for Basic Research into Anthroposophy

PFEFFINGER WEG 1 A CH-4144 ARLESHEIM, SWITZERLAND
www.wegmaninstitut.ch

The Ita Wegman Institute for Basic Research into Anthroposophy is a non-profit research and teaching organization. It undertakes basic research into the lifework of Dr. Rudolf Steiner (1861–1925) and the application of Anthroposophy in specific areas of life, especially medicine, education, and curative education. Work carried out by the Institute is supported by a number of foundations and organizations and an international group of friends and supporters. The Director of the Institute is Prof. Dr. Peter Selg.